To James Landes
dear friend and
great leader –
I am so grateful you
could be here for my
retirement.

Vernon Elmore

April 27, 1986

Man as God's Creation

LAYMAN'S LIBRARY OF CHRISTIAN DOCTRINE

Man as God's Creation
VERNON O. ELMORE

BROADMAN PRESS
Nashville, Tennessee

4216-36

ISBN: 0-8054-1636-6

Dewey Decimal Classification: 233

Subject Heading: MAN (THEOLOGY)

Library of Congress Catalog Card Number: 84-20502

Printed in the United States of America

Unless otherwise indicated, Scripture quotations are from the King James Version of the Bible.

Scripture quotations marked (NIV) are from the HOLY BIBLE *New International Version,* copyright © 1978, New York Bible Society. Used by permission.

Scripture quotations marked (RSV) are from the Revised Standard Version of the Bible, copyrighted 1946, 1952, © 1971, 1973.

Library of Congress Cataloging in Publication Data

Elmore, Vernon O.
  Man as God's creation.

  (Layman's library of Christian doctrine; v. 6)
  1. Man (Christian theology) I. Title. II. Series.
BT701.2.E46   1986   233'.5   84-20502
ISBN 0-8054-1636-6

Foreword

The *Layman's Library of Christian Doctrine* in sixteen volumes covers the major doctrines of the Christian faith.

To meet the needs of the lay reader, the *Library* is written in a popular style. Headings are used in each volume to help the reader understand which part of the doctrine is being dealt with. Technical terms, if necessary to the discussion, will be clearly defined.

The need for this series is evident. Christians need to have a theology of their own, not one handed to them by someone else. The *Library* is written to help readers evaluate and form their own beliefs based on the Bible and on clear and persuasive statements of historic Christian positions. The aim of the series is to help laymen hammer out their own personal theology.

The books range in size from 140 pages to 168 pages. Each volume deals with a major part of Christian doctrine. Although some overlap is unavoidable, each volume will stand on its own. A set of the sixteen-volume series will give a person a complete look at the major doctrines of the Christian church.

Each volume is personalized by its author. The author will show the vitality of Christian doctrines and their meaning for everyday life. Strong and fresh illustrations will hold the interest of the reader. At times the personal faith of the authors will be seen in illustrations from their own Christian pilgrimage.

Not all laymen are aware they are theologians. Many may believe they know nothing of theology. However, every person believes something. This series helps the layman to understand what he believes and to be able to be "prepared to make a defense to anyone who calls him to account for the hope that is in him" (1 Pet. 3:15, RSV).

Contents

1
The Mystery of Man

Who is man? Where did he come from? Where is he going? These and like questions have plagued the human mind from the earliest times. Man is a mystery to himself. He is still trying to put the pieces of the puzzle together and provide for himself a satisfactory answer. A recent author began his autobiography by saying, "I left home at the age of sixteen, looking for me." From ages past the human race has been in search of itself. The subject has been explored through art, religion, myth, poetry, and philosophy. When our early ancestors sketched an image of the human hand on the wall of a cave, they were expressing fascination with their own uniqueness. All peoples have created legends to explain their origin. Archaeologists digging in the mounds of Mesopotamia found clay tablets upon which were recorded a creation epic that had some points in common with the Book of Genesis. The legends of Greece and Rome sought to account for the human race as descendants of the gods. Shakespeare exclaimed in *Hamlet*, "What a piece of work is a man! How noble in reason! how infinite in faculty! in form, in moving, how express and admirable! in action, how like an angel! in apprehension, how like a god!"

Diversity of Opinion

The Bible affirms this lofty opinion of man. It characterizes him as made a "little lower than the angels" (Ps. 8:5). On the other hand, many students of human life today avow that he is scarcely above the other animals. It seems that we're not any closer to resolving the dilemma in our time than were the ancients. The diversity of opinion concerning human origins is accented almost every day in the newspapers. The conflict over the content of science textbooks and the subject matter of classroom lectures reflect the fact that we're still having difficulty making up our minds about the identity of man. Scientists theorize, and religionists dogmatize, and n'er the twain shall meet.

There are obvious differences between people and the rest of the animal kingdom. Otherwise, the question about human uniqueness would never arise. The very fact that the human can recognize and reflect upon these differences identifies him as a superior creature. Someone has said that man is the only animal that talks to himself. New schools of investigation have been developed to explore the human frontier, such as anthropology, archaeology, and psychology. Scholars are probing mounds, mores, and minds, trying to provide solid answers to the question, What is man?

The Uniqueness of the Human Species

The Human Soul

Benjamin Disraeli, the English statesman, once asked, "What does make humankind different from all other living beings?" We're still asking that question and attempting to pinpoint particular aspects of humankind which make it unique. A very early answer focused upon the concept that the human has a soul. Descartes saw a clear-cut distinction between humans and other living creatures. He said that animals are mechanical automations; they lack consciousness and feelings. Although the human body is a living machine like the body of an animal or plants, he said, the difference lay in that people possess a soul. In other words, there is a spiritual identity to humanity. There is a reflective and reverent dimension to human nature. During the age of rationalism, the religious content was downgraded and human uniqueness was identified as the rational mind. He was given the scientific name, Homo sapiens or wise man.

Toolmaking and Language

Benjamin Franklin noted that the distinction lay in the fact that humans were the only tool-using animals, while others have indicated that the uniqueness of the human being lies in his ability to manufacture tools. Many anthropologists have contended that language marks the distinction between human beings and other animals. Most animals are able to produce sounds and establish a kind of communication in this way. A recent study revealed that seals have a vocabulary of more than thirty-five different sounds which they use for various purposes, such as sonar or expressing their emotions in certain situations. The songs of insects like the cicadas, crickets, and katydids are utilized in mating calls. Birds and mammals utilize sounds to warn intruders away from their territories. Bees have an intricate system of communication to share information about food sources. Animals have alarm signals when danger approaches.

Human language is a phenomenon, however, much more intricate and sophisticated. It is not simply a feeble device to serve elementary purposes as in other animals. Ideas and information can be shared through a system of word images which are symbols for various objects, actions, and thoughts. The construction of the human mouth, throat, and ear and the specialized development of those parts of the human brain related with our speech facilities set man apart.

The Limited Capacities of Animals

Research into animal behavior, however, has in recent years revealed that certain animals do have limited capacities in some of the areas considered distinctive of human beings. Jane Goodall, in her study of chimpanzees and the great apes, has showed us pictures of these animals utilizing simple tools. The California sea otter employs a stone to free mollusks from rocks and then to crush the shell. The definition of human beings as the only tool-using animals has had to be revised. Furthermore, chimpanzees have been trained in the laboratory to communicate by the use of American sign language, by arranging plastic disks, or by using buttons on a computerized control board. They demonstrate, therefore, an elementary capacity to reason and communicate. One chimpanzee, after years of intensive training, learned the gestures for a hundred or so words in the American sign language. The human child by that time, however, would have a vocabulary of many thousand words and could combine them into a huge number of grammatical patterns.

In fact, if language were the only distinction between the human being and the animal world, then what could we say about our remote ancestors? Did they have facility of language? They left no record, of course, to fortify our assumption. No single attribute elevates man above his fellow creatures. We know that the primitives made tools. They could kindle fires. They were self-conscious because they drew crude pictures of themselves upon the walls of caves. They buried their dead, showing a reverence for life. They left behind religious symbols, which reflect a spiritual awareness, also a belief in afterlife.

While the chasm between people and other animals may not appear so great as it once did, still the enormous gap is there. No other creature approaches the capacity of Homo sapiens in intellectual ability, facility with tools, and cultural attainments. There is a vast gulf between the creature who is able to propel himself to the moon and the creatures who live within the strict limitations of their environment and ancestral patterns. The human alone has the capacity for abstract thinking and the analysis of complex things. Mankind alone has the intuition and the ability to preserve his intellectual accomplishments and to build upon this accumulated wisdom. Man is like the animals, but he is a very special kind of animal.

Is Man, Then, Simply a Specialized Animal?

Traits in Common with Other Animals

We have seen that biologically the human is an animal. He has traits in common with other creatures. He has a similar bodily structure and functions. He is subject to disease and death like all other animals. In view of this, the human is often discussed and described as simply a sophisticated animal. Is that which sets him apart his large brain or his erect posture and consequently his free forelimbs which make possible the fashioning and use of tools? Is there nothing more? Has a person been fully accounted for when he is dissected upon the medical student's laboratory table? This is the only view that purely physical scientists can take when they study human life. The spiritual aspects of man are not confirmable in the laboratory nor observable in the man on the street. But is man simply an ape with trousers? A chimpanzee with a college degree? Is he an animal that got the intellectual jump on the rest of the creatures?

A little more than a hundred years ago, not even the scientists would have answered that question in the affirmative. People steeped in the biblical tradition and having no evidence to the contrary believed that the human being, from the beginning, was a different kind of creature.

Dilemma Created by Darwin's Theories

Young Charles Darwin's life was headed for the ministry when he boarded the *Beagle* for its five-year voyage to South America. Along the way, Darwin explored the flora and fauna and pondered the fossils of long-extinct creatures. What he observed on that voyage not only changed his life but also changed the thinking of man about himself. Darwin was bewildered by the peculiarities of certain animals which seemed strangely adapted to their environment. In the Galapagos Islands, for example, Darwin saw that each island had its own distinctive kind of finch. The beaks of the different varieties seemed to be naturally adapted to the kind of food which the bird ate. Now he wondered, *Did God make each finch different, and were they always that way, or has nature redesigned each finch in keeping with its natural inclinations and food supply?* He gradually began to believe in the mutability of the species. Creatures can change across long periods of time to meet the demands of their environment or else they perish.

When Darwin returned home and meditated upon the implications of his theory as related to the human species, he emerged with an idea which shook the foundations of the prevailing biblical concept. In 1859 he published his ideas in a book called *The Origin of the Species.* It was like a bombshell in the religious and intellectual arenas. The battle was immediately begun between the defenders of the faith and the exponents of this new exciting theory of evolution. People had taken for granted that rabbits had always been rabbits and monkeys had always been monkeys and that people had always been people just like they were being experienced in current life. Darwin insisted that living things are not bound in a fixed system. Across the eons of time there have been gradual changes in everything that has a bodily structure. These changes are progressive in nature from the lowest forms of organic life to the higher. The human race is the highest achievement of nature, the apex of the evolutionary process.

Did Man Evolve from a Lower Form of Life?

In Darwin's theory, therefore, man was not created by God as he is, but he evolved from some lowly creature to his present state. Because of the structural and functional similarities between the human being and the anthropoid apes, it is supposed that they came from a common ancestor. Darwin confirmed the idea that mankind is a biological species. Our remote ancestors were not humans but animals. God becomes superfluous in this theory, for evolution is the result of natural causes which do not imply intelligence or purpose. Evolution accounts for the mental and moral endowments of man as well as his physical structure.

Theologians and preachers were panicked by these novel ideas that seemed to threaten the biblical concept. The wife of one clergyman exclaimed, "Descended from the apes! We hope it is not true, but if it is, let us pray that it may not become generally known." Great debates took place between those who were offended by Darwin's theories and those who began to champion them. Scientist T. H. Huxley was Darwin's most daring exponent in England. In America, Harvard's noted naturalist, Louis Agassiz, strongly defended the divine creation position. He could not shake off the teaching he had received as a child in the manse. The battle is almost as lively today with the current controversy over textbooks and teaching procedures in the classroom. There is an insistence that the creation concept be taught alongside the evolutionary theory. Many feel that to do this breaches the separation of church and state and ignores the scientific evidence.

Man Viewed as an Animal

Darwin's ideas seemed to wipe out all distinction between the human being and the animal. Man is an animal and just an animal. There is no clear boundary between Homo sapiens and the animals from which he sprang. The full application of this theory is fatal to the assumption that mankind has a higher spiritual nature. It negates any belief in personal survival beyond death. With the popularization of the theory of human evolution, the scientific systems have tended to study man as purely an animal. It is commonly thought and taught today that we can come to understand much about man by studying animal subjects and then to generalize about human nature. Some people claim that, since there is a great deal of similarity between man and other primates, we are justified in drawing conclusions about people from the behavior of our animal kin.

The scientist Thomas Huxley, although a great exponent of Darwin's theory, toward the end of his life wrote an article for a magazine, saying that he knew of no study which is so utterly saddening as that of the evolution of humanity. He said that, in the theory, man emerges with the marks of his lowly origin upon him. It makes him a brute, only more intelligent than other brutes. Bertrand Russell, the philosopher, once said, "Mankind is the outcome of the accidental arrangement of atoms." The biblical view, of course, transcends this idea that man is simply a biological phenomenon. A grave injustice is done to the human being when he is said to be identical with the other animals. Mankind will never be properly understood from a strictly materialistic viewpoint.

Darwin's Theories Challenged

Some science textbooks acknowledge our limitation in the study of human life. *Christianity Today* quoted the following introductory statement: "This unit, in general, is about what many scientists have thought about the beginnings. Their ideas are interesting and exciting. But since evidence is lacking, people are still left to wonder just how it all began."[1]

As a matter of fact, Darwin's theories are being challenged today as a result of further scientific investigation. A new theory called "molecular drive" was described at a recent meeting of the American Association for the Advancement of Science. This theory maintains that the changes in animal populations occur first, and then they seek a new environment where they can take advantage of the change. The theory is based on the discovery that all human and animal genes are constantly subject to rearrangement. Stephen Jay Gould, Harvard biologist, has said that the theory is radical but probably correct. The scientific world is still restlessly seeking answers to the age-old questions.

Concept of Karl Marx

A producing animal.—Karl Marx, the father of Communism, was greatly impressed with Darwin's ideas. As he sat in the British Museum reading room, pondering over the plight and prospect for humanity, he adopted the view that mankind had developed in the beginning from his tree-climbing ancestors and would in the future develop into something else unknown. The primary thing about man, as far as Marx was concerned, is that he is a producing animal. He employed Benjamin Franklin's definition of man as a toolmaking animal, who consciously and purposefully produces his means of subsistence by changing his environment. Unlike animals who live by instinct, the human is a rational being who is capable of technical achievement. Human beings master nature, whereas the animals merely use it. Marx described man as being a product of four factors: first, his economic needs; second, his tools; third, his environment; fourth, the social organization of his labor. He was contemptuous of all doctrines of human rights and human equality. Mankind has no inherent significance or value beyond his contribution to the well-being of society. Ideally, he said, there would be a complete identity between the individual person and the community. In other words, people exist for the community, and it is only here that they find their identity and worth.

We can easily see that Marx's philosophy undercuts any concept of the spiritual nature and value of man. He employed evolution to explain the superior human capacities and to eliminate any idea of his uniqueness as a creature of God. The Marxist doctrine of the human being simply as the servant of society undergirds the Communist ideology and is espoused by millions of people in the world. This, of course, suppresses human individuality and freedom. Communism sponsors a mechanical and utilitarian viewpoint of mankind. The elemental fallacy of Communism lies in this very inferior understanding of man. It disdains the individual and justifies the regimentation of people for the purpose of the state. The person is given a very low priority while the community is everything. We are like a colony of ants in that we exist solely for the welfare of the whole colony. Our ultimate responsibility is not to God but to those who run the state.

Man Remains an Enigma to Himself

What were our ancestors like?—The idea that the human race emerged from some primitive ancestor has impressed itself upon the public and is rather generally accepted. An expression of this was a recent movie called *The Ice Man.* Scientists making explorations in the far north accidentally found a Neanderthal man frozen solid in the ice. They were able to resuscitate the creature out of the past and to observe him for a time. Although a rough-hewn version of humanity, he still possessed distinctively human qualities, such as elementary speech and religious awe. It was a fascinating effort in a popular way to say something about man. We all wonder what our remote predecessors were like. Would they be just like us or sport beetle brows and walk in an apelike posture? Since we can actually observe them only in fantasy or through their scant remains, we are still very much in the dark.

Study of primitive cultures.—Further efforts have been made toward the understanding of the human species by the study of primitive cultures. Anthropologists have roamed the world in quest of tribes untouched by civilization. They have felt that by living among these simple people they could gain insights into man's basic nature. For example, Margaret Mead wrote a classic work sharing her observation from a long relationship with the Samoans. Since her death, another anthropologist has challenged her conclusions, saying that she read into Samoan behavior her own preconceived ideas. Back and forth go the arguments about human identity.

Darwin was fascinated by the wild and naked people he found inhabiting remote Tierra del Fuego. He managed to bring back to England on the *Beagle* a young brother and sister, whom the crew named Jimmy Button and Fuegia Basket. They were very celebrated persons, as the British were anxious to see if such savages could be introduced into civilized behavior. They became, therefore, a kind of national experiment. They learned to speak a fragmented English. They were dressed in the latest styles of the day and taught to eat with proper manners. They were schooled in the rudiments of Christianity. Finally they were presented to Queen Victoria at court. They were very lonesome, however, for their own people and were returned to Tierra del Fuego, accompanied by a missionary. It was thought that they would be a civilizing and Christianizing force among these crude natives. Instead, Jimmy and Fuegia immediately took off their clothes and reverted to the primitive life-style. Civilization had not really taken with them. So the experience left the English people even more confused about humankind.

The identity of man remains a mystery which has never been resolved to the satisfaction of all. There is a concensus that, physically, the human is an animal, sharing characteristics common to the other creatures of the world. That he is a superior animal with capacities which far exceed those of any other animal is readily evident. The comparison of the linguistic and toolmaking abilities of some animals to the human facility is almost like comparing a candle to the sun. The gulf between the human and other animals is impassable.

Greek and Roman ideas.—The Greeks and the Romans long ago recognized that man was very special, but they weren't sure in what respect. They recognized that he had inner reflections, intuitions, and rational capacities that set him apart from the rest of the animate world. He functions in a realm that is outside the purely physical. They realized that the human is not just an animated body but a living spirit. They felt that he had a psyche or spirit that continues to live after death of the body in a ghostlike state in Erebus, the gloomy underworld. The Romans shared some of these ideas but did regard the dead as, in some sense, divine beings to whom worship was due. The dead played a part in the affairs of the living. Christianity, of course, reinforces that idea of an eternal spirit. There are at least two functions of man which accent his uniqueness in the creaturely world.

What Is It that Makes Mankind
Superior to the Other Animals?

Obviously, it is not that we have the most advanced bodily structure. We cannot see as well, for example, as some other creatures, such as the birds of prey. Our sense of smell is not as keen as that of dogs, nor is our hearing as sensitive as that of some animals. We do not compare in stamina nor physical strength. We cannot run as fast, jump as high, nor digest food as well. The real superlatives are related to the mental and spiritual capacities of man. Of paramount importance are the two which I will now mention.

Self-awareness

Aristotle once said, "All men by nature desire knowledge." Man's insatiable curiosity about his world and, more significantly, about himself sets him apart. Humans are the only animals who try to discover just what sort of animal they are. Man knows that he exists and is curious about his identity. He is the only animal that asks the questions How? and Why? He ceaselessly investigates himself, exploring the world of his consciousness, and seeks to understand himself in relation to other human beings and to his environment. He records his past and anticipates his future. He is a self-determining creature who decides what he will be and what he will do. Somebody has said that the human is the only creature who knows that he is going to die. He contemplates his own death and that of others. Self-consciousness leads to self-appreciation. Usually people have reverently buried their dead. In finality, the human being can love himself.

God Awareness

Man, the self-aware creature, is also sensitive to the existence of a higher self. He has a capacity for self-transcendence, in that he can look beyond himself to a higher identity which he has perpetually quested. He has instinctively reached out to this greater self in a sense of wonder and awe. He realizes that this unseen reality beyond himself is also larger than himself. Mankind at worship reflects an intuition that goes far beyond the animal nature.

When Helen Keller's teacher, Anne Sullivan, finally broke through the darkness and silence to communicate with the little girl, Helen's parents were very concerned that she be told about God. So the distinguished Episcopal minister, Dr. Phillips Brooks, was asked to come and reveal to Helen the existence and love of God. When he had completed his explanation through the teacher, Helen indicated a startling insight. She said, "I always knew there was such a Person but didn't know His name." The experience of Helen Keller is an example of mankind's intuition for God.

Malcolm Muggeridge has beautifully characterized this innate awareness of God in the following words: "Whatever may happen to the nightmare utopias of the twentieth century, whether they materially destroy one another or metaphorically fall into one another's arms, however deep the darkness that may fall upon the world, of one thing we may be certain: in some forgotten jungle a naked savage will feel impelled to dab a stone with colored mud and prostrate himself before it, there opening yet another chapter in man's indefatigable quest of God."[2]

In 1984 *Newsweek* magazine reported the discovery of a seventeen-million-year-old fossil in Kenya. The fossil predates the time when the two lineages of apes and humans were supposed to have branched apart. The specimen was about half the size of modern man and tentatively identified as Silvapithecus. Based on dental evidence, it appears much less simian than Proconsul, the creature previously considered a likely progenitor. A University of Michigan anthropologist said, "We have gone from a more apelike common ancestor to a more humanlike one." "Perhaps," the article concludes, "the apes will have to get used to the idea of descent from man."[3]

A few years ago there were discovered some tracks that had been impressed in the muddy shores of an ancient lake bed. The mud had long since become rock. The tracks were of three individuals, possibly parents and a child. The footprints were very like those of humans today. Perhaps the scientists will never reach any final conclusion about the human nature and how he came to be. Nevertheless, we have at least two tracks that indicate a great deal about man: his self-consciousness and God-consciousness.

Notes

1. *Christianity Today,* Nov. 7, 1980, p. 64.

2. Malcolm Muggeridge, "The Fearful Symmetry of Freedom," *Christianity Today,* April 21, 1978, pp. 887-900.

3. *Newsweek,* April 23, 1984, p. 49.

2

In the Image of God

"Man is an accident." A well-known anthropologist voiced this conclusion as he delivered a television lecture on the nature and origin of man. As we have seen, his viewpoint expresses the popular conclusion today among many students of humankind. They insist that Homo sapiens evolved from some primitive form of life according to the natural processes. He is simply a more sophisticated form of animal life than the rest of the animate world. The Christian understanding of man as a special product of God's creative genius cuts directly across this naturalistic interpretation. The Bible is the basis of the Christian conviction, whereas the anthropologist draws his conclusions from his observations of nature and the ancient human remnants which he discovers here and there.

A few years ago a book was published, entitled *In Search of Adam*. It was an account of man's quest for his primitive ancestors. A diligent search is being made in the canyons and cliffs of Africa for bits of skull, a few teeth, a pelvis of manlike creatures who roamed that area a few million years ago. Perhaps the quest could be centered more profitably closer to home, in human nature itself. We descendants of Adam bear the mark of our remote ancestors. The Bible speaks of it as the image of God in man.

What Is Man?

The psalmist asked, "What is man?" (Ps. 8:4). The question reveals that thoughtful people long ago were puzzling over the human race. Even the ancients realized that man "is fearfully and wonderfully made." As he investigates himself, he demonstrates his uniqueness.

He feels impelled to ask, "Who am I and where did I come from? What makes me different from other creatures?" Philosophers, theologians, and scientists have mulled over these questions. The effort to explain human life has spawned religions, philosophies, legends, sagas, and scientific theories. In college classrooms, science laboratories, pulpits, endless books, and television lectures, the human being continues to try to account for himself.

The Search Goes On

No doubt the search for man will continue into the indefinite future. Physical evidence is illusive and subject to various interpretations. Within the past decade, ideas about the age of man have greatly changed. The date for the emergence of Homo sapiens is being pushed further and further back into time. The Christian is not particularly concerned, however, with the age of man but with the ageless man. It is not to bones but to the Bible that we turn to discover truths about mankind in all the ages. Here are the insights into human nature that unravel the mystery of mankind for us. While some consider this approach simplistic and naive, it provides the most adequate understanding of the complicated and marvelous creature known as man. While other theories denigrate him and reduce him to a mere animal status, the Bible reveals him as a superior creature with the imprint of God upon him. The Christian believes that there is no realistic comprehension of mankind apart from this relationship to God. The human will always remain an enigma and a mystery to those who view him simply from a naturalistic standpoint.

Kinship with God

Conscientious efforts are being made to reflect man's kinship with the apes. It is high time to emphasize his kinship with God. Is there no more to the human than the chemical elements which constitute his body? Is man just a delectable arrangement of atoms? an accident of the evolutionary process? The psychologists have realized for some time that there is a spiritual dimension to human nature. They've gone probing in the dark recesses of the human psyche trying to find what makes man tick. Freud led us into the substratum of human personality. He caused us to see there is an invisible aspect to humanity. He tried to answer the psalmist's question, "What is man?" by exploring this unknown realm of the inner life.

These extrabiblical inquiries into human identity have their place and importance. All such efforts, however, fall short if they fail to take into consideration the biblical account. The Book of Genesis, for example, gives a better comprehension of our personhood than will ever be found in all this collective manhunting. The study of humanity without considering the Scriptures is like studying light without considering the sun. All other sources of information are secondary to the revelation in God's Word. Here alone is provided the key to our self-understanding in the words, "In the image of God created he him" (Gen. 1:27).

A Special Creation

The Main Creative Event

According to the Scriptures, man is not an accident but a special creation. People have importance above all the rest of animate existence. They are indeed a part of the animal world but not confined to it. This distinctiveness of human life is what some people want to deny or to explain away. We do ourselves a great disservice, however, when we think of man simply among the herd of animal life rather than the herdsman. Human life, according to the Bible, was created in a climactic finale to the creative week. In a sense, all the rest of creation was stage dressing in preparation for the main event, the appearance of the star. God crowned His creative activity with the presentation of man. All the other things which God made seemed to be waiting in anticipation for humanity to step on the stage. In the light of the Scriptures, people are not a potluck product of the natural processes. They were specially designed on God's drawing table as a supreme expression of His creative ability. They were purposefully produced by the Heavenly Father to fulfill a preordained role in His world. We are not, therefore, a happenstance but were made by God's own special pattern. We owe not only our lives but also our peculiar qualities as human beings to God and His wisdom. The implication of this truth will be examined in these pages.

The Creation Account in Genesis

Science silent about origins.—The first words of Geneses are, "In the beginning." Only the Bible can speak about beginnings because it is a revelation from God. In other words, in the Bible, God, the Author of all that is, tells us how the world got started. Since He was the only observer at creation, He alone is competent to describe the introductory events. Science cannot really speak of origins because it deals only with things as they are. The scientists can explore the past through the visible remains and draw conclusions and make learned guesses. But the scientist is dealing with processes, not origins. In fact, the scientific discipline can never make authoritative statements about beginnings. They can only theorize, for when the scientist becomes dogmatic about things that are beyond his realm of observation, he has invaded the arena of faith. The scientist can neither affirm nor deny the biblical doctrine of creation because it is a proposition we accept by faith. No one can ever prove that God created the world. God told us He did, and we believe His Word. Therefore, the person seeking a materialistic answer to the question of origins will go on searching. The solution to the puzzle will never be found. But to the believer, the Bible provides the most satisfactory explanation because it harmonizes with reality as he experiences it.

Two choices.—The Bible says, "In the beginning God created the heaven and the earth" (Gen. 1:1). If that is not a fact, then we are hard pressed to explain how this planet and this universe got here. We have a world on our hands, and obviously it came from somewhere. Ordinarily the naturalistic stance assumes its existence and doesn't try to deal with how it came to be. Since matter does not generate itself, the only other explanation apart from creation is that the world has always been. The universe is eternal! That staggers the imagination. It seems to me that it requires much more faith to believe that the universe is eternal than to believe in an eternal God who spoke it into existence. I believe that there are the two choices: eternal matter or creation. The theologians used to talk about God creating the world ex nihilo, that is, from nothing. Only God could do that, and this is the biblical viewpoint. There is no way to shrug off the Genesis account with intellectual honesty until human genius has produced a better explanation of origins, which is not likely to happen.

Creation Completed in Man

The rest of creation preliminary.—According to Genesis 1, the creative activity of God ceased when He made man. It was as though God saved the best until the last. Creation was a procession of creative acts culminating in human life. Everything else was preliminary to this climactic finale. It appears that the earlier creation would have been incomplete without the introduction of the human species. Man is part and parcel of the natural world but also stands aloof from the rest of creation as its summation and crown. Without people, nature would have been like a sentence without a subject. It would have been like assembling an orchestra without music or having a farm without a farmer. There would have been order with no one to recognize it, beauty with no one to appreciate it. "It is good," God said when He had completed each day of creative activity, but there was no one to applaud. "It is very good," said God when He made Adam, for here was the one creature who could say back to him, "Amen."

The world created for man.—Man's superiority to all the rest of creation is somewhat like God's superiority to man. The world is not simply man's environment but his dominion. God's instruction to Adam and Eve and, thence, to their successors was to subdue and have dominion over the other creatures who shared their habitation. Human life was not an afterthought of God but a forethought. Genesis reflects that God created the world for mankind. He already knew the kind of creature man would be and supplied him with a habitat suitable for his welfare. Some modern theories see mankind adapting to its environment, but the Bible portrays God adapting the environment for the benefit of man. The Bible, then, bestows upon humanity a dignity and providential purpose which all other views fail to comprehend.

In the Image and Likeness of God

"Let us make man in our image, after our likeness" (Gen. 1:26). The human race is a specialized creation of God, unique among all the rest of earthly creatures. This distinctiveness is implied in the decision of God to create mankind in his own image and likeness. No real understanding of man can be achieved without probing into the significance of those two words, "image" and "likeness." What a sterile study to try to understand people by comparing them to the primates! True understanding must be found in comparing the human to his divine Author. Even so, there has been a great deal of speculation through the centuries as to the significance of the terms "image and likeness of God."

Meaning of the words "image" and "likeness."—Some Bible scholars have tried to make a distinction in the meaning of "image" and "likeness." For example, image has been considered the essential nature of man as God's special creation. The likeness was thought of as reflections or characteristics of this image, such as goodness, grace, love, and the like. It was taught that, in his fall, man retained the image but lost the likeness. It seems, however, that the two words are intended to identify the same phenomenon, and the repetition is meant for emphasis. The Hebrew word for image is *selem.* It refers to a hewn or carved image (see 1 Sam. 6:5; 2 Kings 11:18), like a statue, which bears a strong physical resemblance to the person or thing it represents. The word *likeness, demuth,* means a facsimile (see 2 Kings 16:10). Mankind, therefore, is a kind of carbon copy of God. "Likeness" is a sort of verbal trailer echoing the meaning of image. Neither of these words implies that man is divine. He was endowed with some of the characteristics of God; he was not made from a purely material mold. There are qualities about man that can only be understood in the light of this divine endowment. In his human nature, he is more like God than he like the rest of the creatures. He is more than bones, brawn, and blood. His physical traits are only the visible facade, not the complete self. He does not live simply by instinct but by insights that are denied the other creatures. The psalmist had in mind this uniqueness of mankind when he poetically described man as made "a little lower than the angels . . . crowned with glory and honour" (Ps. 8:5).

Likeness but not sameness.—While the words "image" and "likeness" imply similarity to God, they also denote the radical difference between God and man. There is a likeness but not a sameness. Genesis 5:3 says that Adam became the father of a son in his own likeness and after his own image. In other words, his son Seth was a human being with traits and characteristics of his father. When one saw Seth, one was reminded of his father, but he was not his father. He was a distinct person with an identity of his own. A few years ago a movie was produced about Will Rogers. His son portrayed his father in the film. Will Rogers, Jr., looked a great deal like his father, talked like his father, and did an excellent job of displaying characteristics of his father, but he was not his father. Mankind has a kinship with God and, in many ways, resembles God, but the difference is distinct. Man is man, and God is God. God is always the Creator and man the creation. God is the Spokesman and man the word. But there is a living relationship between the word and the Spokesman.

What is the likeness?—In what sense is man created in the image of God? The Bible does not give us a systematic development of this subject, so across the ages the theologians have wrestled with what they called the *imago dei* in man. Since the Scriptures do not define it, the matter is open to human speculation, and there are naturally many different views. There will probably never be an absolute consensus on the matter, but there are aspects of it we can recognize and in which we can glory. I think it is very important to explore the matter if we're going to have any adequate self-understanding. Furthermore, this biblical and Christian concept is being severely challenged today by those who think of man as just another animal. Impressive books on human origins are constantly being published. He is being called "The Naked Ape." In the classrooms, mankind is being interpreted on a biological basis. Many of these students of human nature have theological blind spots which prevent them from considering man in the fullness of his being.

Is the likeness physical?—Many years ago I heard an elderly Sunday School teacher say that he believed that God is just like man. "After all," he said, "The Bible speaks of God as having arms, hands, eyes, heart, and other physical features." One religious group today believes that God and Jesus Christ have bodies of flesh and bones just as man, no doubt basing their doctrine on the image of God in man. Since man is in the image of God, God must also be in the image of man, a physical identification. Is this what is meant by the Genesis passage?

Michelangelo painted on the ceiling and walls of the Sistene Chapel in Rome a panorama of the creation, the fall of man, and the Flood. God is shown in the act of creating Adam. A close examination of the image of God reveals a startling fact. The face of God bears a remarkable likeness to that of the artist. It appears that Michelangelo, whether by design or accident, protrayed God in his own image. We must be wary of creating God in our image, a reverse psychology which is the opposite of what the Scriptures teach. Jesus once said, "God is a Spirit" (John 4:24), and it would naturally follow that the image of God in human life would include spiritual aspects.

Reinhold Niebuhr has said that, because man is made in the image of God, man is unable to be satisfied with a God who is made in man's image. The human has the capacity to look beyond himself sufficiently to know that a projection of himself is not God.

Anthropomorphism.—The attributing to God of physical characteristics in the fashion of man is called anthropomorphism. This means speaking of God in human terms, such as the heart of God or the eyes of God or of God walking and talking. We do this in order to have some grasp of His person, nature, and activities. God is so far beyond our ability to comprehend that we must assign to Him some familiar features in order to talk about Him. When we say that God sees, however, we do not mean that He has eyes like ours but that He knows what is going on. In theological terms, this refers to His omniscience. God is all-knowing. Most of us recognize the difference between the spiritual and the physical realms and are not apt to associate the image of God with the mere physical characteristics of man.

Man, a Living Soul

In Genesis 2:7 we read, "The Lord God formed man of the dust of the ground, and breathed into his nostrils the breath of life; and man became a living soul." It is evident that something special happened to man when God created him, which was not true of the other creatures. It is never said that God breathed into the animal's nostrils so that they became living souls. God endowed mankind with a unique quality of life often identified as the immaterial aspect of man, his spiritual nature in contrast to the physical. Frequently, therefore, man is conceived as having two parts, body and soul. He is a soul living in a body. This is called a dichotomy or a division into two sections that are quite separate. Those who have held this view believe, therefore, that the image of God resides in the soul.

This implication cannot be drawn from Genesis 2:7 without distorting what is said. The author wrote that God animated Adam's body and endued it with a special quality of life. Man became a living person with a self-conscious, intelligent existence. The passage does not say that man *has* a soul but that he *became* a soul. Therefore, this refers to man as a human being, with all its implications. In his humanness, man is both body and soul or, more accurately, he could be described as body-soul. Without either body or soul, man would not be man. James Orr put it like this. "The idea in chapter two, verse seven assumes that man's body, the organic frame, was produced by God by whatever processes from lower elements and that, through the inspiration of the Almighty, was imparted to or awakened within the newly created being that higher life which makes man what he truly is, a personal, self-conscious, rational, and moral being."[1]

The human being, therefore, is neither just a physical being nor a spiritual one. He is both at the same time. He is an entity, body and soul. This is called the holistic view of man. Somehow, therefore, the image of God must relate to the total person whom God created.

The Old Testament view of man.—The Old Testament supports the holistic view. Man was considered a unity. He was not segmented into separate parts known as body, soul, and spirit. The human being as a whole is the created work of God and is in the image of God. The

Platonic view of man as a spirit living in a body was not a view of the Old Testament writers. They may have spoken of man as soul or spirit or reins or heart, but it is the person in his entirety that they were thinking about. A particular term was utilized when the writers were emphasizing some aspect of a human life. For example, when the author was speaking of the life or the individuality or strong desire, *soul* was the word used. *Spirit* was the word employed when eternal influences or a power above the individual was being accented. *Heart* usually had reference to the intellect, will, and conscience. *Reins* often referred to motives. These words do not identify some distinctive compartment of the human being but some expression of his personality.

There are many facets to human nature, but they are all integrated into one total person. When the psalmist said, "No man cared for my soul" (Ps. 142:4, KJV), he was lamenting that no man cared for *him*. It was not some spiritual dimension of his life that no man cared for but his entire self. In Hebrew thought, man is an animated body. It is through his body that man is localized, visualized, and socialized. He was created with the capacity to relate both to his physical environment and, also, to God.

Spirit and soul.—The word *spirit* (*ruach*) in the Old Testament means "wind" or "breath." It is used interchangeably in the Old Testament with *nephesh* or soul. The spirit is not considered a more exalted state of man but is related to the unity of body and soul. In Genesis 2:7, where the Bible speaks of God breathing into this clay corpse called man, it obviously does not simply mean that God animated him. Into no other creature did God breathe this breath of life. It must mean that God bestowed upon man a spirituality unknown to the other creatures. In other words, the human being is not just a physical animal but has a spiritual nature, which makes possible his fellowship with God. He is spiritual as well as physical, and both aspects constitute the full self.

The human is a specialized creature with spiritual characteristics that enable him to embody the attributes of God. The spirit in man is concerned with his selfhood, self-awareness, all the elements of

personality, in contrast to the pure animal existence of other creatures. The possibilities of self-realization, as well as communion with
God, are inherent in man's spiritual nature. Man is not man in his
mere physical organism; he is a living person (soul) with physical and
spiritual attributes. Man can be a person because he has spirit. Spirit
is what makes him transcendent over and distinctive from the rest of
the animal world. Those who say that man is just a sophisticated
animal have a very partial and immature view of human nature.

Viewpoint of Early Theologians

Influence of Greek Philosophy

Many of the theologians in the early days of Christianity were
greatly influenced by Greek philosophy in their interpretation of the
image of God in man. Plato employed the terms *image* and *likeness*
in his teachings. The real world, as he saw it, was the invisible or the
spiritual, of which the visible world is simply an image. Physical
objects are an imperfect reproduction of their counterparts in the
spiritual world. He spoke of the immortal spirit of man in distinction
from the physical body. In Greek thought, there was a separation
between the material and the spiritual. The philosophers saw man as
a spirit living in a physical body. This Greek dualism was the background out of which the early Christian theologians drew their understanding of man as God's creation. They interpreted the doctrine of
the image of God in man out of the context of the separation between
the body and the soul.

Image of God in the Soul

The church fathers were, therefore, inclined to believe that the
image of God resided in the soul or the spirit of man. True selfhood
is found in the enduring soul, rather than in the transitory body. The
spiritual capacities of man reflect a kinship with God. Irenaeus said
that Christ was the primordial image after which man was created.
When Jesus came in the flesh, He presented the ideal image of man
as God meant man to be. Irenaeus made a distinction between image
and likeness. He said that image refers to man's nature as a rational

and free being; likeness, on the other hand, related to man's moral character. This likeness was lost in the fall of man but is restored when he becomes conformed to the image of Christ through the work of the Holy Spirit. The image of God in man is never lost.

Augustine maintained that, since God is a Trinity and has a three-fold expression, so we must look for a trinity of traits that reflect the image of God in man. He said that the first trinity is that of mind, knowledge, and love. The second trinity is meaning, intelligence, and will; the final trinity, the remembrance of God, the understanding of God, and the love of God.

Later Theologians

The Body Disdained

Later theologians followed the cues of their predecessors in associating the image of God with the spiritual aspects of human life. Thomas Aquinas thought that the image of God was found in the intellect. Man has the natural capacity to know and love God. This capacity is inherent in every being so that the image, therefore, is found in the soul as it turns to God and responds in love to His person. The early fathers, as well as their intellectual heirs, therefore, emphasized that the image of God was seated in the soul, which they identified with the spiritual part of man. The role of the body was downgraded. Such an attitude was consistent with their background in Greek thought. This interpretation was the fountainhead from which flowed the idea of asceticism, or the denial of the body. Since the body only served a temporary function and was of secondary importance to the soul, it became a religious virtue to severely discipline the body. The physical functions and bodily demands were considered to be distracting to one's spiritual welfare. For the image of God to flourish in man, it was essential to subdue the flesh. Martin Luther, in his spiritual struggles, reflected this conviction. He punished his body by wearing a hair shirt next to his flesh and by lashing himself. The monastic establishment which magnified the simple life-style was, in part, a product of this idea of the image of God in the soul of man.

John Calvin, the great Reformer and father of Presbyterianism, taught that the image lies primarily in the understanding, or, as he said, in the heart and soul. While not denying the importance of the body, he maintained that it could not be a part of the image. The body shows some reflections of God's glory but does not share in the image.

Modern Theologians

Man Is Totality

For the most part today, theologians have rejected the Greek influence and have returned to the Hebrew idea of man as a totality. Image of God, they feel, is found in the whole person, rather than simply in the spiritual aspects. The human being is no longer viewed as a dichotomy (body and soul) but as a unity (body-soul). Man is an embodied soul; therefore, any consideration of humanity must deal with the whole person. The human is a diverse creature with bodily and spiritual characteristics united in oneself. He cannot be segmented and said to bear the image of God in one part of his being and not in the rest. Body and spirit belong equally to the nature of man. Neither is to be subordinated to the other one. They are designed and destined for each other. Water is constituted of two elements, hydrogen and oxygen or, as we write it, H_2O. Eliminate either hydrogen or oxygen, and you do not have water. In a similar way, man is comprised of both body and spirit. Eliminate either of them, and you do not have man.

Since man cannot be partitioned as a soul temporarily imprisoned in a body, the entirety of man must, somehow, be in the image of God. The body gives to the individual localized expression. Through the body he relates to his physical environment, just as in spirit he relates to God. Because he has a body, he is able to communicate, learn, and express personality. He makes contact with his world and with other human beings. It is alien to the Bible to think of the body as an inferior product and as an embarrassment to the soul since the body is in the image of God as well as the rest of his being. The body should be treated with dignity and not considered the seat of evil and to be looked upon with contempt.

Current Trends

Body of Little Value

There is a popular trend to look upon the body today from the same viewpoint as the Greek philosophers. The body is considered simply a physical vehicle for the convenience of the true self, which is spiritual. Even in Christian circles communicating the biblical concept of the whole person is difficult. I suspect that the majority of Christians think of themselves as a soul inhabiting a body and that, at death, the real self departs from the body like an eagle departing from her nest. The body that is left behind is no longer of any value and had nothing to do with the essential personhood. It is not surprising, therefore, to see people overindulging or abusing their bodies, feeling that what really matters is the care of their souls. It is a matter of indifference how they treat their bodies as long as they go to church and say their prayers.

An emphasis upon the care of the body would be appropriate in our churches in view of the doctrine of the image of God in the total self. Christians should avoid falling in with the irreverent attitude about the body reflected in the growing opinion that, upon death, the body should be disposed of with as little ceremony as possible. Furthermore, the doctrine of the bodily resurrection needs to be taught, for it reflects the fact that the body is a precious and integral part of the person.

Overemphasis on Physical Fitness

In contrast to those who place little value on the body are those who think of the human being as a physical organism with spiritual aspects. The modern emphasis upon physical fitness and the lack of concern for man's spiritual well-being is indicative of this inadequate viewpoint. No doubt the stress upon health care is needed. Proper diet and exercise are in keeping with the concept of the sacredness of the body. It is sad, however, to see people intent upon keeping their bodies toned up but letting their spirits sag. To think that one is in great condition when he has his body in good shape is a very inadequate understanding of man.

What, Then, Is Distinctive About Man?

Who Is Man?

What is it that sets man apart from all the rest of God's creation? In what way is he superior to the other animals that God placed on the earth? Is he indeed just a sophisticated beast, set apart by his superior intellect and physical adroitness? The natural history books almost universally classify the human race in this category of a superior animal. No credence is given to the biblical identity of man as a special feature in all the natural pageantry.

Rather than asking, What is man? we might more appropriately ask, Who is man? He is not simply an object amid all the other objects on earth. The Bible portrays him as a subject, a self-conscious, willful, innovative entity who, under God, presides over his environment. He acts rather than reacts in his circumstance. While he bears a similarity with the physical features of other living animals, he is special in that God created him in His own image and likeness. According to the Scriptures, he is a "living soul" (Gen. 2:7).

Key Word: *Person*

The point has been stressed that the image of God relates to both the physical and spiritual aspects of man. Is there some key word that sums up the significance of this characterization? I think it is the word, *person.* God made man a person in the likeness of His own personhood. Nothing else in all the creation can be called a person. God endowed humanity with the unusual features of His own person, and these attributes distinguish man from everything else God made. I think, when the Scripture says that man became a living soul, the word *person* could be substituted for "soul." Soulhood implies personhood. Personhood encompasses man in his entirety, body and spirit, as a rational, loving, responsible, moral creature, who in many respects is a mirror image of God himself. Personhood is that characteristic which makes possible a relationship between God and man.

Man, then, is an animal in that he has the same bodily characteristics of other animals. Man is a creature, for God created him. Certainly he is more than an animal and more than a creature. He is not God, but neither is he fully identified with the creation. He is unique in his kinship both to God and creation. He bridges the gap between God and His world. It is tragic for people to see themselves only as creatures and fatal for them to aspire to be God. Made of this earth, man is earthly, but he is not a thing. God animated him in a special way so that he became a living soul or person. Humanity has a relationship with God not granted to the other creatures.

Note

1. James Orr, *God's Image in Man and Its Defacement in the Light of Modern Denials* (Grand Rapids: William B. Eerdmans Publishing Co., 1948), p. 45.

3
Facets of Human Personhood

The highest possible compliment to the human race is the scriptural characterization of man: "created . . . in the image of God." This statement constitutes an impassable gulf between mankind and the rest of creation. People have a dignity and an identity which relegates them to a superior role in earth's population. We have defined the image of God in man as his personhood. Man is a person, as God is a Person. Man's uniqueness as a person is immediately observed in his self-awareness and his God-awareness, two features that are foreign to the other animals. In this chapter, I will elaborate a little further upon some of the aspects of man's personhood. He is a multifaceted creature who must be viewed from many angles to observe the full glory of his divine image. I will not exhaust the list of his unusual qualities but call attention to some of the more important ones. These characteristics are suggested, first of all, by implication from the personhood of God and, secondly, from the observation of man. We may legitimately ask, What is God like? and then draw from our answers reasonable conclusions about humanity. This image of God in man is not an abstraction but is realized in a concrete way in man's personal makeup.

Individuality

No Two Alike

God is an individual. He once said, "I am that I am" (Ex. 3:14). God has His own identity and existence separate and apart from His creation. Man created in God's image is also individual. Individuality is that which distinguishes the person from God and other people. The Federal Bureau of Investigation recognizes and takes advantage of this factor in the fingerprinting process. No two sets of prints are exactly alike, which accents human individuality. Parents, of course, recognize that each of their children is a person in his or her own right. No matter how much they are alike, they are still different. Ying and Yang were the original Siamese twins. Bound together by a ligament of flesh, they were identified in popular thinking as one person. Nevertheless, they were so distinctive in their personalities that they often disagreed to the point of fighting each other.

For many years my wife and I had identical twins as our neighbors. They lived side by side with their separate families. They told an amusing story about the time when one of them took his wife to a beach resort for a few days. The next week his brother, who was newly married, took his bride to the same resort. The manager was greatly confused and spoke confidentially with the new bride, saying, "I hate to tell you this, but your husband was here last week with another woman." Despite their near physical sameness, they were, nevertheless, distinct individuals.

To Each His Own

Each human being has identity and uniqueness. One cannot be cloned or duplicated. Persons are separate entities with individual personalities, sets of values, inclinations, and responsibilities. Every human is an original with private relationship to self, to others, and to God. This factor has significant implications in the redemptive plan of God. People are not saved en masse, but the Lord deals with mankind one by one. When God comes seeking us, He asks, Where are you? God dealt with Adam and Eve separately in respect to their personal disobedience.

As an individual, the human being is a self-determining creature. God gave His instructions, but Adam and Eve chose to disobey them. Humans are free to set their own course and determine their own life-styles. Other creatures are captives to their instincts. Theirs is a largely predetermined pattern of life. The human can exercise a discrimination in his daily behavior unknown to other animals.

The Bible reflects this individuality by the giving of separate names to Adam and Eve. They had an identity independent of each other. Though bonded into an intimate relationship, each one thought and acted upon personal inclinations. Each in his or her own little world was, in a sense, as sovereign as God in the larger context.

Rationality

The first man and woman are portrayed in the Bible as rational creatures. The serpent appealed in a subtle way to Eve's reasoning faculties and pressed upon her a decision. Adam and Eve were thrown into a mental and moral dilemma. The argument of the serpent seemed very logical, as well as catering to their natural instincts. The consequence was an unfortunate action, revealing that man is governed by his rational faculties, as well as being conditioned by his animal instincts.

When God came seeking Adam and Eve, they hid from Him with the explanation that they were naked. God asked, "Who told you that you were naked?" (Gen. 3:11, RSV). Of course, they needed no one to tell them. They were equipped with the ability to analyze their situation and to comprehend their nakedness. No other creature on earth would be so aware of its peculiar circumstance. The human is not only self-conscious but self-critical.

Rationality as the Image of God in Man

Some of the early Christian writers were so impressed by human rationality that they claimed that human reason is the image of God in man. This one thing, they maintained, was what distinguished people from the other creatures. They realized that no animal possesses the power to reason in the fashion of man. Therefore, rationality, they said, is what makes man superior. While man shares with other creatures the animal nature, it is the ability to reason that makes him human and gives him his distinctiveness. Christian thinkers like Augustine and Calvin agreed that the ability to reason constituted the image of God in man.

Only One Characteristic of the Image

In actuality, while reason is a phenomenon uniquely characteristic of man, it is only one aspect of that divine image. Rationality corresponds to the biblical image of God as a rational Being. The orderliness of the universe is reflective of the rational mind of God. It would be expected that, if God made man in His own image, He would bestow upon him His rational nature. The human ability to analyze and reflect, even upon abstract matters, is suggestive of his unusual heritage from God.

Is this the only attribute, however, associated with the image of God? William L. Hendricks maintains that this would mean that those of a greater intellectual endowment and perhaps more formal education would be more in the image of God than others.[1] The truth is that all men are created in the image of God regardless of their particular intellectual prowess.

Man Is a Thinking Animal

Nevertheless, the rational nature of man is certainly an important part of the divine image. Man is a thinking animal who has facility for reflecting upon himself and his environment. He has the capacity of unraveling knotty problems and of projecting solutions to dilemmas. His intelligence is creative in that it allows him to improve his environment, to rise above his natural limitations. While animals must have a favorable habitat to survive, the human can turn thorns and thistles into a productive environment.

Robert St. John in his book *Ben Gurion* tells of the accomplishments of an energetic man named Sam Hamburg. Hamburg left Palestine for America after World War I and studied agronomy. He became a legendary figure for his success in turning California desert into good cropland. On a visit to Israel, Hamburg told Prime Minister Ben Gurion that fine crops could be grown in the wastelands. He asked for some desolate acreage upon which to prove his point. He was assigned six hundred acres in the Bet She'an Valley of Galilee, two hundred feet above the Jordan River. It was yellow, parched land covered with weeds and wild pigs. "How are you going to get water up to this level?" he was asked. He replied, "God and me, we'll do it together." He planted ten acres of cotton on his model farm. He appeared one day at Ben Gurion's office with an entire plant in his hand. It was a luxuriant proof of his proposal to make the desert bloom.[2]

Thrust from the garden to live by the wits God gave him is the story of mankind. Man has the exceptional ability to learn by experience and to apply what is learned to future situations. He can make decisions and draw conclusions. He can analyze observable reality and theorize about the invisible. He can vocalize his thoughts in an intelligible way to other rational human beings. His remarkable intellectual abilities affirm the fact that he was made in the image of God.

In a Class by Himself

Thomas A. Edison developed an intelligence test which he gave to all his prospective employees. He called it an "ignorameter." For most of us, our ignorance quotient is considerably greater than our intelligence quotient, yet the superiority of humans in this category is remarkable and suggestive of the divine touch. The comparative intelligence and reasoning powers of other animals have been tested. Surprisingly, it seems that the common pig rates very high among the animal intelligensia. Man is in a class by himself, however, when it comes to rationality. Even though some scholars feel that our cerebral excellence is simply an evolutionary triumph, the evidence points to the fact that the intellectual potential of human beings has always put other animals in the shade. When the anthropologist goes searching for ancient man, he looks for tools and other indications of superior skills. No other animal is able to solve the simplest mathematical equation. No other animal reflects upon his own identity or destiny. It seems that other creatures live largely by their instincts, whereas Homo sapiens exists in the realm of rationality.

Spirituality

A little girl once took a note from her mother to her physiology teacher, saying, "Dear Teacher, I don't want my Mary to learn anything more about her insides." In order to know more about ourselves, we have to look on the inside. Physiology can't tell us all there is to man. The Bible takes for granted that there is a spiritual side to the human being. God never walked and talked with the other creatures. There was something peculiar about man which made possible this two-way communication.

More Than Physical

When we look on the inside of ourselves, we are conscious of an existence in addition to our physical bodies. There is more to me than just my fleshly parts. I have an identity independent of my body. This is what the Bible teaches when it says that God formed man from the physical elements but that man was not complete as yet. God breathed into his nostrils the breath of life "and man became a living soul" (Gen. 2:7). This unique personhood of mankind is more than a creature of flesh and blood. We have a spiritual nature that is part of our heritage as created in the image of God.

"God is spirit" (John 4:24, RSV). Thus did Jesus characterize God in his conversation with the woman at the well. She had been talking about a God with physical limitations who dwelt in a certain locale. Jesus wanted her to see that the Heavenly Father does not have material characteristics, which is a truth that we should all readily perceive. It also has implications for understanding the image of God in man. Since God is a spiritual person, it naturally follows that the personhood of man must, in some sense, be spiritual. The human being can't be defined by or confined to his material attributes. As God is spirit, so man is spiritual. Otherwise the image of God would not be real. This likeness with God must conform to the nature of God.

It is startling to realize that many of the students of humanity entirely ignore the spiritual identity of man. They consider it so much theological jargon and insist on getting down to the realities. There is a story about a group of medieval scholars who were inquiring about the number of teeth in a horse's mouth. No one knew the answer because the page in Aristotle which contained the information had been torn from the book. One of the scholars horrified his colleagues by suggesting they look in the horse's mouth. One philosopher said, "The proper study of mankind is man." Any proper study should suggest that the human being is not a physical machine but a person with both physical and spiritual aspects.

Makes Possible Communication with God

If man is just a physical entity, he has no facility for communication with God. Before Alexander Graham Bell developed the telephone, he was a teacher of the deaf. He was a diligent student of the voice mechanism. He and his brother once built a replica of the human voice box and, by use of a bellows, were able to produce sounds like "mama." Utilizing his knowledge of sound production, Bell taught some of his deaf students to speak. He could do this because he was dealing with another person like himself with the possibilities of interaction and speech. His students delighted their families and friends by being able to converse with them in a way that a mere machine could never do. In the same way, God can communicate with people and vice versa because of this spiritual kinship.

Scriptures Agree

Christian doctrine assumes that the individual is constituted of both physical and spiritual attributes. Sometimes these two aspects of human nature are in conflict. Jesus rebuked the sleeping apostles in Gethsemane and charged them, "Watch and pray, that ye enter not into temptation: the spirit indeed is willing, but the flesh is weak" (Matt. 26:41). "Flesh" often identifies the physical nature of man in contrast to the spirit; at other times, "flesh" identifies the evil longings associated with man's physical being. Either way, the word indicates a distinction between the body and the spirit of man. Paul admonished, "Glorify God in your body, and in your spirit, which are God's" (1 Cor. 6:20). In speaking of the advantages of a woman remaining single, Paul said, "The unmarried woman careth for the things of the Lord, that she may be holy both in body and in spirit" (1 Cor. 7:34). The Bible is consistent throughout in characterizing the human being as both body and spirit. This understanding of man is foundational to the theme of the Bible, the fall and the redemption of the human race.

Responsibility

A Duty to Perform

Man as a person has purpose. God, in whose image he is created, plays a responsible role in His relation to creation. Human beings were not placed on earth simply to exist or to enjoy their pleasant environment. God gave them the assignment to oversee it. They are answerable to God for the manner in which they fulfill this obligation. Man has a threefold responsibility, to God, to himself, and to the world. Mere existence, in the sense that other animals exist, fills people with a great feeling of frustration and purposelessness. Human life was never meant to be a perpetual "siesta." Human beings seem to feel that their lives must have purpose, and they look about to find their particular tasks.

When people are not cast into some responsible role, they tend to degenerate. There is an inherent need to be something and to do something. We see this reflected in the criminal element in a negative sense. People want their lives to make a difference even if it has to be in social misbehavior. Why, for example, would an Oswald take dead aim at the president of the United States from an upper story window? Some would explain this as irresponsibility. In fact, it was probably his own warped sense of responsibility to make his impact upon the world. People are not content simply to flow with life but to manipulate life in positive and negative directions.

Accountable to God

As a responsible person, God could not simply create man in His own image without bestowing upon him a responsible intuition. Furthermore, humans feel an accountability to God. In a recent movie entitled "O God, II," God (in the form of George Burns) appeared to a little girl. God felt He wasn't getting enough press, and so He commissioned the little girl to come up with some slogan that might attract attention. Finally, she conceived of the words, "Think God." God said that was fine, so she enlisted her friends, and they began to plaster posters everywhere and to write the words on school blackboards, walls, and the like. "Think God." In fact, God has always been in the mind of the human beings, even though they are not always aware of it. In moments of crisis, we cry, "O God!" Though often we try to live without any reference to God, the awareness is buried deep in our inner beings.

A few years ago Marian Anderson, the noted black singer, did a concert in Russia. She was advised by her agent not to sing any religious hymns because it would offend the people. She, in turn, informed him that spirituals were always a part of her repertoire and insisted upon singing them. She concluded her concert with two of her most famous. When she went backstage, the audience was in an uproar. People had rushed to the stage and were shouting in guttural tones, "Heaven! Heaven! Deep River!" Marian Anderson had touched a responsive cord in the hearts of these theoretically atheistic people. Paul on Mars Hill reminded the Athenians that God is not far from any one. This nearness is indicated by that unaccountable urge in human life to live responsibly.

The Need to Work

The other animals are content in life if they have plenty to eat, a comfortable place to sleep, opportunity to play. Most of us feel driven, however, not just from the necessity of making a living but also for the making a life. One man has said, "Blessed is the man who has found his work; let him ask for no greater blessing." Even when people have the affluence to drift through life, they are plagued with a sensation of guilt if their lives are not invested in something that has meaning. This is why we are responsive to calls to duty and assume obligations on a voluntary basis. We are not content to live life on a moving sofa. Man is blessed or plagued with a sense of responsibility.

This feeling of responsibility issues from personhood. Other creatures do not share this call to duty. This is a quality peculiar to man in his humanness. Human existence is responsible existence. This responsible being is monitored by his own conscience and, ultimately, by a sense of obligation to a higher being. The history of mankind is written against the backdrop of this innate sense of responsibility. The customs, laws, traditions, and cultural patterns of the human race are understood only in the light of this inherent quality. It is a law operating in human life as realistically as the law of gravitation in the natural world. To deny or defy responsibility sets man at odds with himself and with his world.

Morality

Capacity for Moral Judgment

When God made man, He deposited him in the midst of a moral dilemma. God said to Adam, "Of every tree of the garden thou mayest freely eat: But of the tree of the knowledge of good and evil, thou shalt not eat of it: for in the day that thou eatest thereof thou shalt surely die" (Gen. 2:16-17). This instruction of God indicates that this new creature was capable of responsible action. The symbolism of the tree of the knowledge of good and evil is that right is to obey God and wrong is to disobey God. Morality is based on the will of God. It was not Adam's prerogative to question why but to obey. All of which assumes that God constituted man with the capacity for moral judgments. Life for the human animal was to be characterized by a constant round of decisions in the area of right and wrong. Each person must live with the consequences of those moral verdicts. When Adam and Eve violated the instructions of God, they immediately felt guilt and fear and sought to hide from God. Disobedience changed their relationship to themselves and God.

In contrast, there is no moral quality about the decisions of the animal world. They do what comes naturally and have no censoring conscience. There is no feeling of guilt on the part of a cat when it claws the furniture. He will proudly bring a still fluttering bird which he has caught to display his prowess to his master. We are horrified at his heartlessness, but the cat feels only frustration when we take the bird away. As humans we are caught constantly in the tension of right and wrong, good and evil, because we are moral beings in a moral context.

The Choice Maker

Morality is closely associated with the concept of responsibility. A responsible being must be capable of making value judgments. Man is a choice maker. He can say yes or no to given situations. He determines his own course of life rather than having it determined for him by nature. He has no coercion other than that of his conscience and his understanding of moral principles. He can just as readily defy his best knowledge of right and wrong as to follow it. Adam and Eve in the garden knew better; they simply did not act upon their knowledge. Most of us *know* better than we *act*. We rationalize our actions and justify them so that we may appear to be in the right. Otherwise, we suffer the agonies of remorse and guilt. Humans are unique in that they alone experience shame.

A Sense of Oughtness

The human is capable of rising to heights of noble idealism. When Socrates was on trial for his life, he could have saved himself if he had been willing to sacrifice his sense of honor. He said to his judges, "A man who is good for anything ought not to calculate the chances of living or dying; he ought only to consider whether he is right or wrong." When God constituted man in His own image, He endowed him with a sense of oughtness. Only the most depraved human beings are devoid of this impulse. This need to do right is a direct heritage from God who is always in the right.

Bearing Responsibility for Choices

Adam and Eve initially were neither good nor bad; they were innocent. They had the potential of moral character, but not until they exercised their prerogative to choose between good and evil did they become sinners. Their fall was both moral and spiritual, moral in that they failed to live by their highest understanding, spiritual in that their action disrupted their relationship with God. The moral dilemma of man is that he has the capability of doing right or wrong, that which is helpful or hurtful, depending upon his inclination. He can obey his highest instincts or follow his most morbid urges. He cannot do so, however, with impunity. To violate moral responsibility brings inevitable judgment in the form of character deterioration and spiritual isolation.

The moral quality of man is such that he is capable of an idealism that supersedes personal, selfish interests in behalf of God or society. There is also the capacity for moral degeneracy as a consequence of violating man's inherent sensitivity to right and wrong. When people act nobly, there is an inner affirmation. When they make improper choices, remorse and guilt plague them. The conscience of man, which is his moral monitor, can be fine honed into a sharp, sensitive instrument or bludgeoned into dull insensitivity. He must bear the responsibility for the moral direction of his life. God did not make him a moral derelict, going where the winds of fate may direct; but he is the helmsman and must chart his own course by whatever may he chooses to follow.

Immanuel Kant, one of the supreme thinkers of modern times, summed up his great thoughts with the following sentiment: "Two things fill me with constantly increasing admiration and awe the longer and more earnestly I reflect on them: the starry heavens without and the moral law within."

Autonomy

Masters of Our Fate

God took a great risk when He created the human race. He gave man the freedom to govern his own life. William Ernest Henley in his poem, "Invictus," talks about man's "unconquerable soul" and concludes by saying, "I am the master of my fate; I am the captain of my soul." This may sound like a belligerent infidelity, but there is truth in that statement. God made man commander-in-chief, sovereign, of his own life. He is an autonomous creature in that he is in charge of his own affairs. He has been set loose to live by his own desires. Alone of all God's creatures, he is self-determining. He is chairman of the board.

God Shares His Autonomy

This autonomy of man is a reflection of the sovereign God who is Lord and Master of His world. When God speaks, all creation listens. God wills and acts accordingly. No one says no to God except mankind. God shared with mankind a bit of His own autonomy. God deliberately imposed limitations upon Himself when He brought into being a creature who was also willful. God does not dictate to man in the sense that man has no alternative. Man is free to choose personal life patterns. God can say to us, "Thou shalt not," but we can respond by saying, "I will not." This freedom to exercise personal discretion makes us human. Man is not a mechanical toy which God turned out in His workshop for His own amusement. He gave man inherent powers that were previously characteristic only of Himself. Right away Adam and Eve exercised their God-given freedom by reacting negatively to God's instruction. They were free to do as they pleased but, of course, not free from the consequences of their actions.

Autonomy Offers Possibility of Fellowship

If man cannot say no to God, he cannot say yes to himself. He would not really be a person but an automaton. God could have created us as robots, but this would have excluded the possibility of fellowship. There can be no meaningful relationship with a robot. Real conversation can take place only between two authentic persons. Fellowship is made possible only by common consent.

When parents see their children off to college, they wonder what kind of relationship they will have with them. The children have now become persons in their own right. Will they, by their own initiative, keep the communication lines open? They are under no constraint other than that of love. Frequently, parents and children enter into a new, mature, and more satisfactory relationship than ever before.

In a similar way, God released man in a world where he was sovereign of his own affairs if he chose. The creative purpose of God included the hope that this free and autonomous person would of his own volition seek fellowship with God. Only in an unrehearsed and uncoerced communication would the creative design be met and the loving intent of God fulfilled. God wanted a relationship with another sovereign person. Because man has authentic, self-conscious identity, it is possible to interrelate with other persons, including the Divine Person.

Mankind's autonomy, then, is the basis for true religion, as well as social involvement. Worship in the real sense is walking and talking with God. The ultimate meaning of man's autonomous personhood is found as he willfully and eagerly seeks communion with God.

Potentiality

Man, the Dreamer

The sons of Jacob deeply resented their younger brother, Joseph. They contemptuously remarked as they saw him approaching, "Behold, this dreamer cometh." They plotted to rid themselves of Joseph by casting him into a pit and cynically declared, "We shall see what will become of his dreams" (Gen. 37:19-20). God made man a dreamer. He equipped him to have visions of grandeur and the power to fulfill those dreams. It is in order to ask of each person, "What will become of him and his dreams?" When Elizabeth gave birth to John the Baptist, the events associated with his arrival caused people to wonder about him and ask, "What manner of child shall this be!" (Luke 1:66). The same question can be asked of every child born into this world, for each one has a great potential for good or evil. The possibilities of man are suggestive of the divine image. God certainly would not have made a creature who could dream dreams without the potentiality of realizing them. He created man with the capacity not only to grow physically but also to grow spiritually in his godlikeness.

Made, but Always in the Making

The human being is a person in transition. He is always becoming something other than what he currently is. In a sense, the other animals are finished products. They come from a mold, so to speak, with a limited individuality and potentiality. Man is always a person in process. I'm reminded of the Sunday School teacher who asked a pupil, "Who made you?" To which he responded, "I'm not finished yet." There is a sense in which people are never finished as long as they are in this world. They have the capacity to change. This is both their glory and challenge because they can change for the better or for the worse.

This alteration in life comes about largely through personal choices, a truth graphically illustrated for us by Adam and Eve in the garden.

David mounted the pinnacle of greatness only to come tumbling down when he yielded to degrading inner urges. All our lives, then, we are caught up in a tension between what we are and what we might become. Abraham Lincoln's mother advised him, "Be somebody, Abe." It almost seems that God perpetually whispers this instruction to us.

We have an inner drive to be somebody. This may take a negative thrust, as observed in the actions of those who seek to assassinate a president. I suspect behind their effort is the need to be somebody, not to leave this world unnoticed. This instinctive need is one of the marks of our divine authorship. The human is endowed with a holy restlessness to make his mark in the world. This is one of the most hopeful aspects of the human personality. It often leads people to devote themselves to great causes. John Milton as a boy felt very strongly that he was in the world for a purpose. He dedicated himself, even as a lad, to long hours of diligent study. He cultivated his native genius to that point where he could give to the world great works of literary art, such as "Paradise Lost" and "Paradise Regained."

The Possibility of Being More

In every age there is always a possibility of a Francis of Assisi or a John Wesley or a Billy Graham. The intellectual, spiritual, and physical capacities of man are astonishing. Each of us can always become more than what we are. In the latter part of his life, Paul recognized this truth as he said, "I press on." He never felt that he had achieved the ultimate. Each time the Olympics are held, records are likely to be broken in various events. It doesn't seem long since Roger Banister astonished the world with his four-minute mile. Now it is a regular accomplishment. We can break our own "four-minute miles" if we have the self-discipline. I think that Pittenger has said it well. "There is a prospective quality about human life, a going on, a moving ahead, and more to be grasped and possessed."[3] The ultimate goal of man's becoming is God Himself. The purpose of Christ's ministry is to help man become all that God gave him the potential of being. "But as many as received him, to them gave he power to become the sons of God, even to them that believe on his name" (John 1:12).

Perpetuity

The Inevitable Hour

God is eternal, and man made in His image is perpetual. God did not design the human being for death but for life. To speak of man as immortal is not accurate. Only God is immortal in that He never experiences death. In contrast to other animals, people know they are going to die. This gives them the advantage of being able to prepare for the day of their death. Great ingenuity and effort has been expended in thrusting back the inevitable hour. Despite the fact that medical science and better conditioning have greatly lengthened life expectancy, still the mortality rate is 100 percent. In Thomas Gray's "Elegy Written in a Country Churchyard," this truth is lamented:

> The boast of heraldry, the pomp of power,
> And all that beauty, all that wealth e'er gave,
> Awaits alike the inevitable hour;—
> The paths of glory lead but to the grave.

But is the grave our ultimate destiny? Because man is in the image of God, he partakes of God's capacity for perpetuity. Unlike other creatures, he does not cease to be when his body dies. The spirit of man, which in life is inseparable from the body, in death returns "to God who gave it" (Eccl. 12:7). This truth is not really discoverable through human effort but has been revealed in God's Word and verified in Jesus Christ.

Instinct for Eternity

Man seemingly is endowed with an instinct for eternal life. He has never been content to believe that life in this world is all. Winston Churchill represents that urgent desire of the human race to live beyond the grave. Lord Moran, in his diary, recorded a conversation with that great leader. Churchill, in his old age, one day said to Moran, "I suppose you believe in another life when we die. You have

been trained in logic. Tell me why you believe such things." Moran
commented that Churchill wanted desperately to believe in something
but did not find it easy.[4]

Universally, the human race has desperately wanted to believe.
Research has been made recently into the experiences of people who
have to all practical appearances expired and then were resuscitated.
Kübler-Ross and others have recorded the statements of these people
in books and drawn conclusions from them pertaining to perpetuation. While this phenomena may seem to validate the idea of survival,
it does not guarantee it, for these people were not really dead. The
spirit had not departed finally from the body.

Biblical Confirmation

If Churchill wanted logic, perhaps the most substantiating argument for continued life is that of man created in the image of God.
God endowed man with a special quality of life somewhat like His
own, which would imply ceaselessness. Since death is a realm we
cannot invade, the verification of this intuition and hope must come
in the Scriptures. As a matter of fact, the Bible teaches that the body,
as well as the spirit, has eternal value. In the resurrection at the
coming of Christ, the body will be revivified in a spiritual sense and
reunited with the spirit.

Notes

1. William L. Hendricks, *The Doctrine of Man* (Nashville: Convention
Press, 1977), p. 48.

2. Robert St. John, *Ben Gurion* (Garden City, New York: Doubleday &
Co., Inc., 1971), pp. 246-248, 260.

3. W. Norman Pittenger, *The Christian Understanding of Human Nature*
(Philadelphia: Westminster Press, 1964), p. 27.

4. Lord Moran, *The Struggle for Survival,* A Conversation from the Diaries
of Lord Moran, *Reader's Digest* Condensed Books, 1966, 3, p. 152.

4

Man's Unusual Capacities

Many years ago I purchased in the Holy Land an Alexander the Great coin. It bears an image of the mighty warrior adorned with the horns of the god Ammon. When Alexander led his conquering army to Egypt, the priests received him with adulation and confirmed that he was, indeed, divine, a son of the god Ammon.

Ancient Supermen

In the Greek and Roman mythologies of antiquity, certain persons were said to have been sired by the gods. They were individuals of astonishing abilities, actually ancient supermen. This was the only way they knew to account for these outstanding personalities. As offspring of the gods, it was expected that they would perform mighty feats. Certain rulers were considered to be gods in the flesh. They were literally worshiped by some of their followers and called "theos" and "augustus." Shrines were set up where their subjects came to pay homage. On his first missionary journey, Paul was instrumental in the healing of a man at Lystra. Immediately the people reached the conclusion that Paul and Barnabas were gods come down in the likeness of men. They called Barnabas, "Jupiter," and Paul, "Mercury."

According to the biblical account, God endowed one creature with His own image and likeness. What kind of a creature would you expect that to be? Surely one that far exceeds in natural capacities all the other created entities. If an animal, he would be a superanimal with superlative characteristics which significantly set him above and apart from the rest of the animal world. Created in the image of God, he certainly would have intellectual, moral, and spiritual endowments far beyond that of other creatures. He assuredly would not be an animal who lived simply by instinctive reflexes and whose goal was mere existence. In other words, you would look for someone just like man.

Accounting for Man

We must somehow account for the superior aspects of man's person and existence. Some do so by saying that the human is the result of a long process of evolutionary change from a lower to a higher animal. It is rather bewildering, however, that of all the animals, mankind should have succeeded so signally in the evolutionary process. No other creature begins to approximate the capacities of the human being. It is an impossible leap from the instinctual to the spiritual level of existence. The biblical explanation resolves the matter for those who accept the validity of man's origin in the special providence of God.

A few years ago an anthropologist named Johannsen found in Africa the substantially complete skeleton of a tiny homonid, a man-like creature, which he called "Lucy." Lucy was about three feet tall and, says Johannsen, apparently walked upright. He feels that Lucy was a kind of missing link in man's evolutionary transition from beast to the human being. It takes more than skeletal similarity, however, to constitute a human being. I would be interested in knowing whether Lucy could talk or rationalize or worship. Such attributes seem to be characteristic of man from the most primitive times. His personhood cannot be fossilized for future generations to observe. He has native abilities, however, which are readily detected and suggest that God made him in a special way.

The real "missing link" in the quest for human identity is the biblical revelation of man's origin. Without this understanding, the human mystery will never be resolved. Scientists will go on searching in the debris of yesterday but will never be able to present that semihuman who marks the transition from beast to man. It doesn't exist; for, from the beginning, human life was distinctive and reflected attributes that are unknown to mere animals. As follows, we will consider some of those unusual capacities.

Adaptability

Adapting to His Environment

Man has the capacity to adapt himself to various conditions of life. This truth is illustrated in the Genesis account. Initially, God placed man in an ideal environment, a veritable paradise. Life was easy and good. His wants were readily met. However, in his disobedience, he was thrust from this earthly Eden to a harsh environment where he had to make his way by the sweat of his brow. He soon accommodated himself to this thorn-and-thistle existence and continued to thrive. In some ways, man is less prepared to cope with his environment than most of the other creatures. Without fur or feathers to protect him, he comes naked into the world. He is not endowed with many of the animal instincts which enable the wild kingdom to survive. His God-given mechanicism for survival is his intelligence. He is equipped with the wit and the will to adapt not only himself, but also his environment. In the garden, he sewed fig leaves together for a covering. He can survive under circumstances so alien that other creatures would perish. Almost every nook and cranny of this planet is inhabited by man. He does not need a specialized habitat as do the animals. He has invaded the frigid polar world. He has probed the depths of the sea. He has walked on the moon.

In recent years, a hardy group of Englishmen went around the world from top to bottom. They traversed greatly different geographical areas. They scorched through deserts and sweated through jungles. They crossed mighty rivers and compassed oceans. Most severe of all was the bitter cold of the Arctic and Antarctic, but they pressed on to be the first human beings to reach both poles in a single venture. No other creature on earth could have accomplished such a feat but the human being. He can tolerate vast extremes of heat and cold. He nourishes his body with an extensive menu of foods. He is not nearly so specialized in his diet as other creatures. He has invaded realms which are entirely unsuitable to his existence.

Jacques Cousteau has taught us how to use underwater breathing apparatus so that we can startle the fish in their watery world. My wife has recently taken up scuba diving and delights in photographing the coral reef, a region inaccessible to man's exploration and enjoyment until a few years ago.

We have seen the televised antics of space scientists in their weight-less world. Some of us thrilled to see man's first giant step on the moon. It seems beyond belief that man could project himself to that distant body and could equip himself to survive under such alien circumstances. The conquest of outer space is just another demonstration of the unusual nature of man's inner space. He has a genius for adapting himself to circumstances that are not compatible with his physical construction.

Adapting His Environment

When man has not been able to adapt himself to his environment, he has found ways of adapting the environment to his needs. He has learned to make fire to drive away the cold. He has created his own protective shell in the construction of houses. He has grown crops in barren places by managing the water supply. Today we can dispel the darkness by the flipping of a switch or make ourselves comfortably cool on the hottest days with air conditioning.

When I moved from Kentucky to South Texas many years ago, I almost suffocated with the heat and humidity. Now I scarcely notice until some visitor from the North begins to complain. Roald Amundsen, as a lad, had one ambition, to explore the cold Arctic regions. He sought to prepare for his future expeditions by going on camping trips in the coldest of weather or leaving his window open at night in the dead of winter. He was taking advantage of the built-in human adaptability so that he could tolerate the Arctic chill.

It is marvelous to observe how versatile human beings are in accommodating to their life situations. Surely this is a gift of God's divine foresight.

Adjustability

The Flexible Human

The difference between *adaptability* and *adjustability* may seem to be a linguistic manipulation. I perceive *adaptability* as pertaining to man's capacity to accommodate to his environment. *Adjustability* is a word I'm employing to identify the capacity of man to undergo significant personal changes. The human is flexible in his personal makeup to the extent that his thought patterns, motivations, values, and inclinations can undergo dramatic redirections. Over the past century, students of human nature have been exploring the control factors which determine the course of an individual's life. There was a time when environment was conceived as the major influence upon our destiny. In other words, place a child in the proper environment, and you'll produce a proper child. This theory was exploded in the garden of Eden when God gave to Adam and Eve an ideal setting, but they rejected it. Children growing up in the same household are often quite different in their outlook and behavior. More and more we're acknowledging that heredity plays a significant role in making us what we are. Human beings are preconditioned by their heritage from the past. Each of us has our individualized set of genes and chromosomes from our various ancestors so that we enter this world programmed in the pattern of the past. Not only our physical makeup but also other personality factors are to a considerable degree inherited. This does not mean, however, that our personhood is set in concrete, so to speak, without any possibility of change. This is the glory of man created in the image of God. He is adjustable.

Moral Adjustability

One of the traits passed along by our predecessors is our fascination with sin. We see in the garden that Adam and Eve were strongly attracted to that which was forbidden. This characteristic has been true of every one of their descendants. Even Jesus was tempted to sin; however, unlike all other humans, He did not yield to the temptation. I often illustrate this attraction to sin to children by asking which is easier, to be bad or to be good. Most of them readily recognize that they have to try to be good, but they can just let themselves go and be bad. This suggests that the inclination to sin is very forcible in every human life. Does this mean, then, that man has no alternative but to submit to this proclivity for evil? We've already talked about man's spiritual sensitivity. He has holy aspirations as well as sinful inclinations. By the help of environmental influences and exercise of his own will, he can move his life along a moral pathway. He can also submit to his sinful urges and become a spiritual degenerate.

People Can Change

Irving Stone once described the statesman Henry Clay as a chameleon who would turn any color that might be useful to him. "To read his career," he said, "one must have corkscrew eyes." Indeed, Clay was an adjustable man. People can accommodate themselves to heaven's call or to "earth's slow stain." Character is not static. Human beings can change. If this change is in the negative direction, a person is spoken of as maladjusted; or if positive, well adjusted. People can, also, refuse to adjust. One such unadjusted man was Daniel. He refused to conform to the pagan life-style of the king's court. He declined to eat the royal diet. It was not a matter of stubbornness but strong conviction. If he had violated his conscience, the food would probably have made him ill. Mahatma Gandhi, as a Hindu, was a vegetarian. One day when he was a youth, a Moslem friend persuaded him to eat some meat. He became painfully ill. To adjust or not to adjust is a valid consideration for human beings because that is our prerogative.

Candidate for Spiritual Renewal

This adjustability makes it possible for God's Spirit to deal with man. There is a possibility that he can always change for the better. In New Testament terms, he can be "born again." He can undergo the power of God in such an intense revolution in his inner being, it is as though he were starting life over again. The apostle Paul is a perfect example, for he was completely readjusted on the Damascus road when he met Jesus. He became a new person with new goals and a new direction. This is quite different from adapting to a new set of circumstances. The control systems of life, also, can be readjusted for better or for worse. This God-given flexibility makes man a candidate for spiritual renewal.

Reflection

Reflect Rather Than Just React

The divine image in man is certainly suggested by the fact that we are reflective animals. The human species is the product of God's highest reflection. When all the rest of creation had been completed, "God said, Let us make man in our image, after our likeness" (Gen. 1:26). God made us persons like His personhood, who could reflect and not simply react. God wanted a being of this higher intellect with whom He could communicate. It is said that God walked and talked with Adam and Eve. His relationship with them was unique because they were uniquely constituted in the divine pattern. This gift of reflection enables man to weigh alternatives, devise solutions, choose courses, and change his circumstance. While the beasts follow ancestral patterns little altered from the distant past, man's reflective genius has enabled him to break out of the old cultural molds and to constantly form new patterns.

The writing of this book is a reflective activity. In fact, your reading of it is also an exercise in reflection. As I sit meditating, ideas flutter into my mind, seemingly out of nowhere. Of course, they originated in my deeper consciousness where experience has stored its library. It is phenomenal how the mind can assimilate, correlate, and interpret information, proposing conclusions based upon this mental data. As you read, you are forming opinions about my opinions. It seems God has equipped the human with a computer much more versatile than anything devised by man.

The Thinker

Rene Descartes said, "I think, therefore I am." Thinking identifies human life as a superior existence. Man is the product of a divine

thought, for he came into being by a word. Immediately upon creation, we read, "God said unto them" (Gen. 1:28) This final creature
was one to whom God could speak. Man was a thoughtful, responsive,
and deliberate being much more like God Himself than like the other
animals.

Language

Not only did God speak but also man spoke. Human linguistic
abilities are also the product of man's reflective powers. It is a marvel
that, within every branch of the human race, there has been developed
languages with intricate grammatical structures. People have invented words by which they are able to communicate not only facts about
everyday life but also feelings and ideas. Through the written word,
they can conserve and pass along to other generations the cultural
accomplishments and ideals of their own day. The human being is also
equipped with memory, which provides him with a pool of information upon which he can meditate. He can assimilate and mentally
digest this information, reflecting upon its implications for the present
and evaluating its utility for the future.

Self-Contemplation

One of the distinguishing aspects of human reflection is that of
self-contemplation. Man can mentally look himself in the face and
ask, Who am I? He can appreciate his own personhood and draw a
conclusion about his own identity. Such reflection never disturbs
other creatures. The human knows that he is more than the sum of
his parts. Long ago Socrates said, "Know thyself." Only a creature
with mental objectivity could obey that instruction. This self-knowl-
edge sets the stage for man's understanding that he is not simply a
physical phenomenon but that there are spiritual aspects to his being.
He can, therefore, grasp his identity as a special creation of God. He
has a capacity beyond that of other creatures: man knows that he
knows.

Creativity

Man, the Creature Who Creates

Several years ago I visited a cave alongside a stream in southern Missouri. An uncle told me that he had found some Indian relics around the cave. I noticed a ledge just outside the entrance where it would have been convenient for an Indian to have done chores like cutting up a deer or other animals he had killed. There was a layer of dirt several inches deep on the ledge. I began to sift through the dirt, and presently there emerged a piece of flint about the size of a hand. It had been chipped in such a way that one edge was serrated and sharp. It was a perfect instrument for severing flesh. I was filled with awe as I realized I had come into contact with an ancient representative of the human race. It would never have occurred to me to think that any other creature had left the tool.

Man is not simply a contemplator but a creator. The introductory verse in the Bible says, "In the beginning God created the heaven and the earth." Inevitably, man made in the image of God is also creative. He has an innovative nature. He is not content to accept things just as they are but to make them better. Like God who brought order out of chaos, so man has a genius for improving upon nature. He has a capacity for conceiving new shapes and functions for existing matter. With his hands, he can give form and substance to the symbols in his mind.

Examples of Creativity

The Bible quickly mentions human beings engaged in creative activity, such as tilling the soil to produce crops, dwelling in tents, raising cattle, building cities, handling the harp and the organ, and as an artificer in brass and iron. Man receives intense satisfaction from devising novel and better ways of providing his needs. The primitive man who made the stone knife may have received the same gratification as Edison, who invented the electric light. All of the conveniences of our modern habitat reflect this creative urge and facility which came from God. As I sit in my air-conditioned office, dictating these words into a machine, I am surrounded by the evidences of human creativity. The telephone, for example, is one of the most startling and useful gifts to mankind. This genius for changing things literally revolutionized the life-style of humanity in the past century. No other age of man suggests so eloquently that God invested in the human race something of that marvelous gift of innovation by which He brought the world into existence.

Aesthetic Appreciation

God, the Author of Beauty

It is apparent that God is an aesthete. He was not content simply to create the earth but also to beautify it. There is astonishing beauty everywhere one turns. Elizabeth Barrett Browning said, "Earth's crammed with heaven,/And every common bush afire with God." Nature reflects the comeliness, the form, harmony, and order of God's character. He simply would not have made an ugly world. When He completed His creative handiwork, He said, "It [is] good." The good earth is an expression of God's own gracious nature. The splendor of God is not only reflected in the mighty mountain ranges but also in the tiny weed flowering by the roadside. All creation is beautiful whether considered in its minutiae or in its magnitude. Thomas Jefferson once said, "There's not a blade of grass uninteresting to me." I'll never forget how amazed I was when I first put a slice of geranium leaf under my microscope and saw its cellular structure. I had this same experience when I stood on the brink of the Grand Canyon and drank in the beauty of a sunset. This vast gouge in the earth became an enormous paintpot with ever-changing hues.

Man's Appreciation of Beauty

The fact that, at the Grand Canyon, I was able to appreciate the beauty lavished before me set me apart from the rest of the natural order. The ground squirrel scampering about the cliffs, the buzzards circling above, the jays squawking in the trees nearby, the dog being led on leash, none of these creatures had any feeling for the poetic panorama. They were color-blind to its ravishing splendor. In the

Cave of Altamira in Spain, the tourist can lie on his back and observe upon the ceiling the artistic expressions of his primitive ancestors. Man alone sees this world in its three-dimensional beauty. It is as though God festooned His world simply for human enjoyment. Man alone cultivates flowers and shrubs for pure pleasure. He alone sits beneath the night sky and glories in its spangled beauty.

A Creature to Enjoy It

When I was a seminary student, I took up photography as a hobby. I began with a box camera and have graduated to more sophisticated instruments across the years. Almost magically I began to see the world in a new light. There were pictures everywhere waiting to be taken. I found beauty in an old collapsing barn, in a grain field ready to harvest, in the faces of people young and old. In photography an expensive camera is not nearly so important as a discerning eye. I am very grateful that God gave me an eye not only to see but also to appreciate. I can revel in the wonder of God's workmanship.

Why is it that the human being reacts with exhilaration to all things beautiful? Is it because of his superior intelligence? Perhaps this has something to do with it. I feel that here, again, we find a special endowment of God, corresponding to His own sense of beauty. Only an artist with highly skilled manual dexterity and an eye for beauty can put on canvas a lovely painting. He does this not only for his own enjoyment but for the appreciation of others. God is the original Artist, and the universe was His canvas. With His illimitable skill, He carefully produced His masterwork. He stood back, almost awestruck, at what He had done and exclaimed His satisfaction. There was only one thing missing—someone to enjoy and appreciate His handiwork. As a final act of earth's adornment, He placed in the midst of a garden a creature capable of not simply living in the midst of beauty but of glorying in it. One of those creatures one day exclaimed, "The heavens declare the glory of God; and the firmament showeth his handiwork" (Ps. 19:1).

Discrimination

Quality and Value Judgments

Associated with man's aesthetic appreciation is his ability to discriminate. He can make fine distinctions. He can put things in their relative order. He can tell the difference between things that are beautiful and almost beautiful. Thus, he can evaluate the merit of a painting on the basis of minute considerations. Each person has discriminatory powers, but they are very individual. This accounts, for example, for the differences in taste. One person may like the old masters, while another enjoys the Impressionist school. There are magnificent canvases in either category, but for some mysterious reason, we differ in our aesthetic responses.

Once in a revival meeting in the country, I made the mistake early in the week of indicating that I like pumpkin pie. For the remainder of the revival in the homes where I ate, the wife proudly produced her version of pumpkin pie. The kind I had in mind was like my wife makes, but, needless to say, few of the pies resembled her masterpieces. My palate was offended, and my stomach outraged as I tried to eat with as much gusto as I could produce. Pumpkin pie is not just pumpkin pie. We face these pumpkin-pie situations in every area of our lives: what we eat, the way we dress, our choice of words, the kind of friends we cultivate, the church we attend, the ideals we adopt. All of these reflect our gift and power of discrimination. We can make quality and value judgments that are crucial to our personal development.

Creating a Culture Pattern

When a certain generation or society shares a similar taste, a culture is created. A culture conforms to the level in which the powers of discrimination are refined. Thus, we have different degrees of civilization represented in various cultural groups. Any civilization reflects man's power of discrimination, his ability to draw distinctions and to cultivate tastes.

God, therefore, made man with a capacity to better himself. He can become dissatisfied with old ways when he discovers more convenient or more elevated ways of living. Of course, the power of discrimination can be exercised in a negative way. In the garden, Adam and Eve decided that to partake of the forbidden fruit opened for them new vistas of opportunity and exaltation. Our taste and sense of values depend, somewhat, upon our environmental conditioning. In the presence of an evil influence, Adam and Eve made the wrong choice. This is where education and religion play a formative role in directing the use of these discriminatory powers in a constructive way.

Moral Discrimination

Eden illustrates that man has important discriminatory abilities in the realm of morality. He can observe subtle differences between right and wrong, good and evil. God could have imposed His commandments only upon a creature who could make such fine-line, moral distinctions. The very fact that we can argue the rightness or wrongness of something in the gray area of ethics reveals how we can focus upon the tiniest arenas of morality. Based upon this capacity of discrimination, we can make decisions that ultimately affect our destiny. The classic call of God was given through Joshua to the Hebrew people and is an example of the manner in which God expects us to exercise this power for good. "And if it seem evil unto you to serve the Lord, choose you this day whom ye will serve; whether the gods which your fathers served that were on the other side of the flood, or the gods of the Amorites, in whose land ye dwell: but as for me and my house, we will serve the Lord" (Josh. 24:15, KJV).

Imagination

Conceiving Images

It took a great imaginative power to conceive this universe and bring it into existence. God created the universe, first of all, in His own mind and then spoke it into reality. Where there was nothing, there was now something, something that had existed previously only in God's imagination. Like the divine Author, the human being is also able to conceive in his own mind images of that which does not exist, as yet. Thus, the architects and the artists and the artisans have produced innovative works somewhat in the pattern of the divine Originator. Every child who has ever made a crude drawing, everyone who has ever written the simplest poem, built a box, or produced a garden has demonstrated this most unique gift of imagination. Every manmade marvel first took form in someone's imagination. The Seven Wonders of the Ancient World were simply monuments to man's imagination. We ride in automobiles and airplanes, talk on telephones, watch television without, perhaps, realizing that each convenience we enjoy is a projection of a thought in someone's fertile brain.

The Scope of Imagination

I'm utterly astonished when I stand before a great skyscraper or sweep my eyes along the lines of a vast bridge to realize that these creations were first conceived in someone's mind. Columbus sailed west upon the ship of his imagination and found land. The Wright brothers produced an airplane out of their imaginations. I was pastor of Patillo Higgins, who imagined that there was oil at Spindletop. He kept insisting until an equally imaginative wildcatter drilled and struck the first gusher. Think how boldy some dared to imagine a space journey to the moon! Long ago this quest for the heavens was epitomized in the Tower of Babel. God saw that man's imagination had run wild and that there would be spiritual complications. He said, "Now nothing will be restrained from them, which they have imagined to do" (Gen. 11:6). It does seem at times that there is no limitation to what man's imagination enables him to accomplish. He has often devoted his powers to the creation of that which is destructive, such as weapons of war. That same imagination, however, has produced penicillin and many other things that prolong and make life more comfortable.

Re-creating the Past

Imagination enables us to re-create the past. I will leave soon to take a group to the Holy Land. For the Bible student and sincere Christian, the interest of such a trip is not simply to observe the present circumstances. There would be many more exciting places to visit than the eroded hills of Israel. The thing that gives the journey significance is historic imagination. The modern pilgrim is walking in the footsteps of Jesus and other great biblical persons to whom we owe such a debt of gratitude. A mound of rubble suddenly becomes a walled city around which the children of Israel are marching at the command of God. By imagination, the travelers can hear the trumpet sound, a mighty shout rends the air; and they see the walls of Jericho come tumbling down. The boat upon which they are crossing the Sea of Galilee stops in the midst of the lake while someone reads a passage of Scripture; and suddenly in the mind's eye, they see Jesus walking on the water. By imagination, man has the ability to reconstruct the past. This gives him a historical appreciation and perspective.

Anticipation

A Forward Look

Because man has imagination, he also has anticipation. That is, he can project himself into the future. The serpent appealed to the imaginations of Adam and Eve by suggesting to them that, if they ate of the forbidden fruit, they would be as gods (Gen. 3:5). No other creature concerns itself with what it shall be. The future is a blank because they exist only for the moment. God, who knows the future, has enabled the human race to have expectations and intuitions about what lies ahead. Even as he can summon up the past, man can call forth the future. He can experience on the stage of his imagination a bit of the drama, dread, excitement, and joy of events yet to come. As has already been pointed out, the human is the only animal that knows he is going to die. This alone has dynamic implications in his everyday life. It has the advantage that he can prepare against that day.

As I visited the hospital one day, I was asked to call upon a man who was to undergo severe surgery. He got down to business as soon as I walked into his room. He said, "I want to accept Jesus as my Savior. Tell me how to be saved." In a short time, he had trusted the

Lord. He survived the surgery. In the months that followed, he expressed great peace of mind and personal joy that his destiny was secure. Without the element of anticipation, such an experience would not have transpired.

Planning Ahead

The human being has the creative genius of being able to plan ahead. He can make projections into the future and work toward those ends. In this he reflects the image of the Heavenly Father, who conceived His redemptive agenda long before He created the human race. God moves according to a program which has a present implication and a future culmination in the return of His Son to the human scene.

Man saves for a rainy day. He buys insurance against the likelihood of his getting sick or having an accident or dying. He listens faithfully to weather forecasts and plans the next day accordingly. He can look forward to vacations or retirement. He can map a strategy or plot a course. Anticipation drew Columbus across the ocean blue. Anticipation assembled a group of patriots to sign the Declaration of Independence. Anticipation sent the wagon trains West during the California gold rush.

The Christian Hope

Perhaps the most elaborate expression of anticipation is the conviction of life after death. God has endowed man with an eternal expectancy. The promises of Jesus concerning heaven would fall on deaf ears and unresponsive minds if there were not the factor of anticipation. Only today would matter. Tomorrow would not really exist. What a dull and limited existence with sunsets but no sunrises to expect! The Christian element with which anticipation rewards us is hope. Hope brightens our days because we can look forward to something better than we now know. We can even say like Paul, "To die is gain" (Phil. 1:21). Hope is unique to human experience. Mankind is especially blessed as created in God's image because by memory he can live in the past and by anticipation he can venture into the future.

Affection

Emotional Response to Others

Man has strong sentimental feelings. He relates to other human beings not as objects but as persons. This is in imitation of God who has an attachment to human beings that He never expresses toward the rest of His creation. He sought human company in the garden. He was very interested in the welfare of this person whom He had created in His own image. He responded personally to Adam and Eve's disobedience.

Apparent in the Genesis account is that one of the personal characteristics of man is his emotional response to other human beings. Obviously, Adam and Eve had a unique affectional bond. On the other hand, between Cain and Abel there arose a bitter hostility that led to violence.

Closest Identity with God

Probably man never more completely reveals his identity with God than in the expression of love. Love is the supreme characteristic of God. Our most sublime expression of this is in John 3:16: "For God so loved the world." God shared with humanity the beautiful capacity for caring. Man never more completely approximates deity than in the experience of love.

Affirmative and Negative Feelings

Yet, because man is not God, he is also capable of giving vent to the negative of love, which is hate. Love is not exclusive with man as it is with God. In his relationships with other humans, man responds with affirmative or negative reactions. Carried to the extreme, these feelings can turn to affection or hatred. Affection can lead to friendship, while hatred can vent itself in rejection or violence. Man's godlikeness is most evident in the love relationship.

Responding Love

The only adequate response to love is to love in turn. The one thing which God, who is Love, desires from human life more than anything else is a corresponding love. He created man with this affectional nature, something like His own, so that He could enjoy with him a fellowship of love. Love needs an object of affection which returns that love. John expressed the natural two-way love communication when he said: "We love him, because he first loved us" (1 John 4:19). In the love of God, man most clearly gives evidence of His divine authorship and unique endowment in the image of God.

As we have reviewed some of man's unusual qualities, surely we must admit that he is fearfully and wonderfully made. When God created man in His own image, He equipped him for a life that was unique and superior to that of any other creature. He gave him powers that quickly projected him to a place of dominance in the animal order. It seems to me that no conclusion about man is satisfactory that does not take into account his likeness with God.

5

The Divine Assignment

I grew up in a small town in the Missouri Ozarks. Along the edge of our town was a tiny tree-shaded stream. Some time before I was born, a concrete dam was placed across the stream, forming a small lake. It was a happy place where people of the community came to picnic and to splash in the clear waters. As a boy, I loved to wander along the stream below the dam, fishing in the eddies for brim. But then in the 1930s the scene drastically changed. The city fathers decided to allow a milk condensery to be built beside the lake. The waste material from the condensery spilled into the stream, fouling the waters. The little stream seemed to become embarrassed with its ugliness and stench. The fish were destroyed for miles downstream. No longer did children play in its waters. It was an environmental blight.

Ecology versus Economy

Of course, in those depression days, the condensery was a considerable economic boom to the county. The farmers started building up dairy herds and brought their milk to the condensery. Many young men found employment. There seemed to be little regret on the part of community leaders at the loss of the stream. Here was a case where economy prevailed over ecology. The condensery put food on the table and clothes on the back. What did the death of one little stream matter? Apply this principle, however, on a universal scale, and it does matter in an alarming way.

Man's Responsibility for the Environment

Does man have a responsibility for his environment? Is he free to exploit it in any way he desires? These questions must be answered in the light of the assignment which God gave to man in the beginning. It seems that God designed the human race for a special purpose. In Genesis 1:26 we read, "And God said, Let us make man in our image, after our likeness: and let them have dominion over the fish of the sea, and over the fowl of the air, and over the cattle, and over all the earth, and over every creeping thing that creepeth upon the earth." God spelled out our responsibility toward the good earth in just two words: "subdue it" (Gen. 1:28). The psalmist, also, identified the human responsibility: "Thou madest him to have dominion over the works of thy hands; thou hast put all things under his feet" (Ps. 8:6). God gave the first two human beings an apprenticeship in fulfilling this divine mission by placing them in a garden with the assignment "to dress it and to keep it" (Gen. 2:15). By analogy you might say that the earth is a garden, and man has the task of gardener. He is not simply an element in his environment but is to have dominion over it. God placed him in a managerial role. He is answerable to God for the way in which he fulfills his assignment. God never issues a work order without checking up to see that it is done. We must conclude, therefore, that the manner in which we treat our environment has theological implications.

Dominion Consistent with Image

An Undersovereign

Image and dominion are inevitably associated. Man created in the image of God partakes of the essential characteristics of God. Among these attributes of deity is the sovereignty of God. Psalm 24:1 declares, "The earth is the Lord's, and the fullness thereof; the world, and they that dwell therein." God is the Lord and Master of His world. He created man in His own image with the design that man should be an undersovereign over the created world. God endowed the human race with some of His own capacities for sovereignty. He especially equipped them with a native intelligence, physical dexterity, an ability to accept responsibility, a managerial capacity which enabled them to assume authority over and exercise a creative relationship to their environment.

Other creatures use the environment and often abuse it. The elephant, for example, rips limbs from trees and tears bark from the tree trunk, often denuding the tree and destroying it. The lumbering giant simply goes from one tree to another with no thought of replacing the twisted and torn victim. The earth is for forage and not restorage. The mandate of God to man is not a license to exploit but a commission to guard and keep. The "good earth" deserves good treatment.

I have a tiny garden in which I raise tomatoes and a few other vegetables. It is astonishing how amply the earth rewards those who care for it. It is also amazing to see how quickly the garden becomes a weed patch without proper care. The good earth needs a master who will utilize its productivity and deliver it from destructive forces.

Personhood and Dominion

Some interpreters have suggested that the image of God in man consists in man's dominion over the world. This is an inadequate interpretation, however, because dominion is only one aspect of the human identity. Image, as we have previously discussed, relates to the personhood of man. As God is a Person, so also is the human being, who reflects many of the divine attributes in a minuscule fashion. Only a person can be a sovereign, and only a person can have dominion. Personhood implies dominion, and human beings are superior to the rest of creation as God is superior to His universe, including man.

Stewardship of the Environment

Stewardship is a good biblical word to identify our relationship to our environment. A steward was someone who took care of the owner's property, usually in the owner's absence. God has placed human beings in charge of His vast estate. We must act in the Owner's best interest if we are to be responsible. We must treat the property as the Owner would. The implications of this responsibility are very pertinent to our everyday behavior. Anglican Bishop Montifiore has said that, as stewards and trustees for God, man has an inalienable duty toward and concern for his environment. This duty includes all nature and all life.

An Authority Figure

Lord and Master

Dominion implies authority. As the psalmist said, "Thou hast put all things under his feet" (Ps. 8:6). God has shared with man His own authority. Man is to have "dominion over the fish of the sea, and over the fowl of the air, and over the cattle, and over all the earth, and over every creeping thing that creepeth upon the earth" (Gen. 1:26). In other words, he is the lord and master of creation, looking only to God for his superior. There is a sense in which God has turned creation over to people to to do with as they please, expecting, of course, that they would exercise this authority in a beneficial way. This has not always been the case. Through selfishness, ignorance, and greed, the earth is often abused for man's own gratification. Adam and Eve in the garden quickly took advantage of their status and partook of the forbidden fruit because they saw that it was good for food. Here began the agelong struggle between utility and ecology.

To Enhance Rather than Destroy

Some environmentalists blame our ecological problems upon this religious concept of man in dominion. They insist that mankind should not be conceived as master of the environment but as part and particle of the environment. The idea of dominion carries with it the concept, they say, of being able to do whatever one desires with his environment with no sense of responsibility for its preservation or cultivation. This, of course, is a gross misinterpretation of the idea of dominion. God did give us dominion, not to carelessly abuse but to lovingly tend the environment. The essential idea is that of exercising our human gifts to enhance our world rather than destroying it. Arthur Godfrey once put it like this: "A long time ago, I reached the conclusion that the one contribution a man can make that is truly worthwhile is to leave the piece of ground on which he was nurtured in better shape than it was when he found it." Only in this way do we exercise our authority and fulfill our commission in an acceptable manner.

Growing Environmental Concern

It is true that across the years people have assumed that they had the right to violate and rape the earth if they so desired. Who was to stop them? Nothing except a strong sense of obligation, which is surfacing today in the environmental protection movement. We have been guilty of tearing down our house. Ultimately, *we* suffer the consequences of our own irresponsibility. The fouling of the earth and its atmosphere spells a slow death to mankind. Good Christianity and environmental concern go hand in hand. God put us in command; and when we undo God's handiwork, we alone are to blame.

Caretaker Needed

Every Person a Housekeeper

The word *ecology* has entered the vocabulary of most of us and is defined in the dictionary as the branch of biology that deals with the relation between living organisms and their environment. Ecology descends from a Greek word, *oikos,* which means "house." There is a sense in which man's larger environment is his house. We are given the divine assignment of housekeeper or caretaker of our household, the earth. Many of the furnishings in this household are very fragile. They need careful attention if they are to survive and thrive in the way God intended. God knew that it would not do to build this beautiful house and then to let it go unattended. Therefore, He created and especially equipped a custodian whom He instructed to dress it and keep it. This is a task given to each individual in his own time and cannot be fulfilled by anyone else. In this sense, every person is indispensable. The care of the environment, therefore, is a sacred duty. We are not free to exploit the natural resources with careless abandon or to pollute our environment with indifference or to callously abuse our fellow creatures.

Our church is located on Ocean Drive in Corpus Christi. In such a lovely setting, it behooves the church to maintain its grounds in a careful fashion. Fortunately, we have a man who devotes his time lovingly to this task. All day long he busies himself manicuring the lawn, trimming the shrubbery, tenderly caring for the blooming plants. He has a strong personal feeling about the grounds. He picks up every piece of paper, sweeps the driveways, and receives a joy in his work. He is greatly incensed when someone mars the beauty of our churchyard. The congregation, naturally, has an appreciation and fondness for such a diligent worker. He feels that this is his Christian service. And he is right!

God Cares About His Creation

Not long ago a thief broke into our house while we were at church. Hastily, he loaded into his car whatever he wanted, treating with disdain objects that were precious to us, stealing things that had great sentimental value, acting as though it were his right to claim our possessions for his own. We were offended and outraged that anyone should violate our house in this fashion.

Responsibility to Conserve

I suspect that God also feels quite indignant when we act as though we had the right to treat in an abusive way this earthly house which He created with such loving care. Just as you or I might walk around our home, reflecting with satisfaction upon its comforts and appointments, so God one day gazed upon His completed earth with a great deal of pleasure. It is all very precious to Him, and He expects His caretakers to treat it accordingly. After all, this earth is a finished product. There will be no replacements. The resources of this world are exhaustible. The flora and the fauna are expendable. It is very sad when something with which God furnished our house disappears through human carelessness.

As I am writing, whooping cranes which wintered in the Aransas Wildlife Refuge nearby are winging their way to their summer nesting grounds in Canada. Only a few of these giant birds remain, and they are being watched over carefully by environmentalists. Wildlife conservationists, by plane and ground vehicles, have accompanied these cranes on their northward flight. They are trying to find ways to assist the whoopers in their recovery from near extinction. All of this is done at a considerable expense. Why should we care whether the whoopers survive? I believe these actions are consistent with our human assignment to replenish the earth. We're to preserve the earth in its beauty, usefulness, and fruitfulness.

Attitude of Jesus

In the New Testament times, a school of philosophy known as Gnosticism sought to penetrate Christian thinking. They had the concept that the world is completely alienated from God. Everything in the world is evil. Therefore, God cannot have anything to do with it and cares nothing about it. There is a strain of this Gnostic viewpoint reflected in the actions of those who feel that they are perfectly free to despoil and pollute our environment, that things and creatures are not important to God, and it makes no difference how we use or abuse them. This notion is in complete contradiction to the biblical revelation of God pronouncing a benediction over his handiwork. Furthermore, when God was ready to institute His final plan of redemption, He cloaked Himself with this so-called evil flesh and became a part of this material habitat for thirty-three years. Jesus once said that Solomon in all his glory could not compare to the manner in which God had arrayed the lily of the field. He noted that God clothes the grass of the field and that not a sparrow falls but that God is aware of it. Words like these suggest that our world is watched over with loving attention.

Nature Cherished but Not Worshiped

A wrong attitude toward nature reflects a wrong attitude toward God. Most primitive religions actually worshiped nature. The sun and the moon and the mountains and the rivers and the forests were deified. The gods often took the forms of certain animals which were revered. Near the Step Pyramid in Egypt is the Serapeum, a great underground chamber beneath the desert. It was the burial place for sacred bulls which were mummified and carefully preserved in monstrous stone coffins. In the Hindu world today, this kind of respect is accorded to cows, which wander the streets at will. In America, multitudes of people profess no vital faith in God, but the woodland, the riverside, or the beach is their cathedral. They revel in nature but do not reverence its Author. This world was never meant to be worshiped but to be worked. God is its guardian Owner, and man is the gardener charged to tend it diligently with loving care. That which God cherishes, man should also hold in esteem.

Ruthless Treatment of Wildlife

In their mistaken zeal, some people would literally not harm a flea or squash a bug. Some are conscientiously opposed to the eating of flesh, which deprives an animal of its life. This is a distortion of God's instructions. The Bible says that God Himself clothed Adam and Eve in skins. The biblical assumption is that animals are a part of God's provision for the welfare of man. This would not include, however, ruthless and indiscriminate killing or the harsh treatment of animals. God gave Adam the task of providing a name for the beasts of the field and the fowl of the air. The giving of a name implies that they are creatures of value. Perhaps no more vivid illustration of indiscriminate slaughter is recorded than the wholesale dispatch of the mighty buffalo herds that once roamed the West. Passengers on trains often shot the hulking beasts from the windows in the name of sport. In the past few decades, there has arisen a revulsion against this reckless and cruel treatment of wildlife. Intensive efforts are now being made to preserve endangered species. As a little boy with a BB gun, I would shoot at any bird that would stand still long enough for me to get it in my sights. I remember a man paying my brother and me a nickel apiece for every jaybird we could kill because they threatened his cherry harvest. I'm horrified today that I could ever have had that indifferent attitude. I hope my feelings now are symbolic of a growing realization on the part of human society that our fellow creatures have rights, too, and are dear to God.

Where Art Thou?

Answerable to God

God gave to Adam and Eve the assignment of taking care of the garden. He gave them a rather free hand except for certain prohibitions. This does not mean, however, that they were not supervised. Like any good foreman, each day God came for a firsthand observation and report. One day when He arrived, Adam and Eve were not on the job. In fact, they were nowhere to be found. They had disobeyed instructions and were ashamed to face God. God, therefore, went through the garden, calling, "Where art thou?" (Gen. 1:9). This is suggestive of the principle upon which God operates. He never gives an assignment without an assessment. We are answerable to God for the manner in which we treat our environment. This places ecology in a spiritual context. We have a sacred responsibility to be good overseers of this world. We have a moral obligation to exercise our dominion in a way that would please God.

One of my first jobs as a teenager was in an old-fashioned grocery. I had such responsibilities as sweeping the floors, grinding coffee, waiting on customers, and delivering groceries. The owner was a kindly, old gentleman who had considerable insight into teenagers. He knew that a long, lanky boy would always be hungry and would be tempted by the candy counter. He told me that I was free to eat candy, cheese, bananas, or anything else I desired in the store. He realized that after a few days of snacking, I would soon get used to all this plenty and would practically ignore it. Since he had made me such a generous offer, why didn't I hover around the candy counter and freely partake throughout the day? Because I knew I was under his watchful eye and, though he was generous, he was not foolish. This would have displeased him. I was under a feeling of great constraint to satisfy his expectations.

God's Expectations

God always knows where we are and what we're doing. He has given us a rather free hand but, at the same time, has great expectations. As Christians, we're not at liberty to stand around and gorge on the goodies, disregarding our caretaker responsibilities. There's no sense of constraint like that of knowing that God is perfectly aware of how good a job we're doing.

I believe there is a need for a new emphasis upon the theology of ecology. Christians have felt a great impulse toward soul saving. Why not toward earth saving? Of course, the value of a soul as over against that of a tree or a stream can't be equated. Neither can the care of the environment be ignored. When God gave us dominion, He expected our diligence in protecting, preserving, and enhancing the good earth.

From Garden to Desert

The Delicate Environment

How sad was the plight of Adam and Eve when they failed to exercise dominion according to God's instructions! God, therefore, thrust them from the garden to a thorns-and-thistles existence. The Bible suggests that there were repercussions in nature over their failure. God said, "Cursed is the ground for thy sake; . . . Thorns also and thistles shall it bring forth to thee" (Gen. 3:17-18). Man's sinfulness affected his environment as well as himself. This garden-like environment in which God placed human life is exceedingly delicate. In the beginning, God brought order out of chaos and gave mankind the responsibility of maintaining that order. When we do not handle properly our role as caretaker, chaos quickly takes over again. When our environment is mistreated, it becomes our enemy. Our garden becomes a briar patch which tears at us. The air we breathe will contaminate our lungs. Our water supply becomes liquid poison. Trees no longer provide congenial shade. Our food supply is secretly harboring deadly chemicals. Our world becomes more and more a hostile no-man's-land.

Somebody has said that man has a remarkable capacity for producing deserts. The land of the Bible shows the results of man's rapacity. We are told that the eroded hills of Israel once flourished with trees and vegetation. Across the centuries the trees were recklessly cut down, and the land of milk and honey became comparatively barren.

In recent years, the Israelis have engaged in a reforestation program. Something of the land's ancient beauty and fertility is being restored. In the Jerusalem area around the walls of the old city, a parkway is being created. Green grass, roses, and shrubs cover the scars of neglect and insensitivity. The Valley of Hinnom, once the garbage heap of Jerusalem, now has an outdoor theater and is lush with vegetation.

Survival at Stake

The human race is becoming disturbed about what is happening to our environment. We've been forcibly awakened to the fact that there is not an unlimited supply of everything. Hopefully, we're gaining a new respect for our role as conservers and enhancers of nature. We're becoming alarmed that our thoughtlessness has created a very precarious state for that thin layer of air, water, and soil which supports life on the earth. Our very survival is at stake. Most of our food supply comes from less than 25 percent of the earth's area, and a great deal of it from less than 15 percent. Every year vast acres of that slender segment are being gobbled up with expressways and urban development. There simply is no more land, and we must carefully husband what we have.

Urgency of Care

The Worldwatch Institute, an international research group, reports that some U. S. forests are showing signs of dead, dying, and damaged trees like those found in broad areas of Central Europe. They are blaming air pollution, including acid rain, for this increasing damage. Pollution patterns in America are similar to those in Europe. Germany alone has lost more than one billion dollars in timber. Scientists cite industrial pollutants and acid rain as major contributors to the disaster. The problem, then, is worldwide. In America our "woods and templed hills" may become barren knolls unless something is done. Every year vast acreages of timber are burnt off through a carelessly thrown match or cigarette. It is urgent that every citizen, particularly every Christian citizen, become an informed and diligent member of a world watch to preserve our environment.

At last, the principle of dominion is being incorporated into the laws of the land. Conscientious efforts are being made to clear up pollution, to redeem violated land, to purify waters, and to protect endangered species, and that none too soon.

Rapid Increase in Population

The rapid increase in the world population is making such a move absolutely imperative. Recently the Population Reference Bureau published the latest estimate of the world population: 4.762 billion. This represents an increase of 85 million from last year's estimate. The world increases by nearly three human beings every second. At the present rate of population growth, by the year 1987, it will have reached five billion and will pass the six billion mark by the end of this century. The rapidity of growth is seen in the fact that it took thousands and thousands of years for the human population to reach one billion in 1850. Just eighty years later there were two billion. By the 1970s, the population totaled four billion. Such a vast increase of people could bring utter desolation unless we earnestly face up to the situation. Currently it is estimated that twenty million people starve to death every year. Fortunately, there are signs that the growth rate is beginning to slow as attention is being given to population control. There is a possibility that the figure will stabilize somewhere around eight billion or a little less than twice the current population. The human race has no alternative but to dedicate itself to environmental control.

Time Is Running Out

A cartoon caption expresses the situation ironically like this: "Eventually we will run out of food to feed ourselves, fuel to warm ourselves, and air to breathe. This is something we must learn to live with." Perhaps an even greater threat to man's existence than nuclear war is despoliation. The human race needs to be reeducated and alerted to this danger. Astronaut Edgar Mitchell became an ecological crusader after his trip into space. Viewing the earth from that vantage point, he said he had a feeling that time is running out for us. He observed with alarm our smog-shrouded earth. Every day industrial plants, automobiles, heating systems, and the like are contaminating our our atmosphere. Some days school children in Los Angeles are asked to remain inside at recess lest they breathe the foul air. Acid rain has become a topic of concern in northeastern cities because of the fallout of industrial pollution. Of course, we must have industry, but we must also have clean air; and ways need to be found to prevent this contamination.

Sources of Pollution

Paul Herman Müller of Switzerland received a Nobel Prize in 1948 for proving the effectiveness of a compound called DDT in dealing with insects. Its widespread use has resulted in almost terminal damage to some areas of the environment. The brown pelican, for example, has practically disappeared from the Gulf Coast after eating fish contaminated with DDT. The DDT caused the thinning of the eggshells, which broke during incubation. Experts associated with the Massachusetts Institute of Technology estimated that about one-fourth of the 63,000 metric tons of DDT produced in the United States in 1968 finally made its way to the oceans. DDT was even found in the seals and penguins in the Antarctic.

We are living in the age of the plastics, which have replaced, to a considerable degree, wood and paper. We would hardly know how to get along without plastic cups, bags, utensils, and the like. Yet this seemingly innocent plastic is a considerable polluter. Plastics are not readily biogradable. When discarded, they may last for years. Walk along the beaches, and you will find that a considerable portion of the litter is plastic in one form or another. This indicates that plastics have become a common type of flotsam in the world's oceans.

The joy of going to the beach in Corpus Christi has been considerably reduced in recent years by the prevalence of tar. It is a great nuisance to have to clean the tar off your shoes or feet following such a visit. Where does it come from? While some of it may be natural seepage from the ocean bottom, much of it is apparently a residue of the oil spill from a few years ago off the coast of Mexico. It is estimated that about two million metric tons of oil are introduced directly into the world's waters each year. This comes from oil tankers plying the seas, submarine drilling for oil, and other industrial fallout.

Individual Responsibility

Of course, it is easy to blame the oil industry, big business, urban development, and the like for the disruption of our environmental health. Everyone of us, however, has a responsibility to do our part in the earth's gardening. I was driving down beautiful Ocean Drive here in Corpus Christi, Texas, the other day, and saw someone throw a beer can out of the window of the car. This act is symbolic of the insensitiveness of many people to our ecological problem. They feel free to contaminate, pollute, and clutter. It seems inconceivable that people will litter lovely beaches with debris after exploiting it for their pleasure. What kind of monsters are we that we're so insensitive to this ugliness and show such lack of concern for others? This heap of ugliness grows each year as Americans pile up seven million junk cars; one hundred million tires; twenty million tons of papers; twenty-eight billion bottles; forty-eight million cans.[1]

Violation of God's Trust

How it must have pleased God to have prepared such a glorious garden for man's habitat! *Surely,* thought God, *man will enjoy this and will take care of it.* He, therefore, turned it over to us and put us in charge of its keeping. Too long we have violated this trust. We do honor God when we honor His creation. We must rethink our Christian responsibility to relate redemptively to our environment. Only in this way are we fulfilling our divine assignment.

Some time ago a *New Yorker* cartoon showed a man and his wife looking through the picture window of their living room. Before them lay a beautiful panorama of fields and trees. The man is saying, "God's country? Well, I suppose it is, but I own it." The cartoon vividly illustrates our human confusion between God's ownership and our stewardship. The earth is the Lord's, and we are its caretakers. There is no room for vanity but every reason for humility before such an enormous confidence which God has placed in us.

Note

1. Lynwood Mark Rhodes, "The Ecology Dilemma," *The Kiwanis Magazine,* Sept. 1970, p. 26.

6
Human Dignity

David Ben Gurion, a founding father of the modern state of Israel, used to say that reading the Bible kept him from feeling insignificant. The psalmist asked, "What is man, that thou art mindful of him? and the son of man, that thou visitest him?" (Ps. 8:4). He asked that question in view of all the majesty of God's creation: "When I consider thy heavens, the work of thy fingers, the moon and the stars, which thou hast ordained" (v.3). How puny and inconsequential the human being seems alongside the other natural wonders. Reflection upon the truth of man created in God's image gave the psalmist the insight to appreciate human dignity. "For thou hast made him a little lower than the angels, and hast crowned him with glory and honor. Thou madest him to have dominion over the works of thy hands; thou hast put all things under his feet" (vv. 5-6).

Humans Are Special

The dignity of man is derived, not inherent. God bestowed that dignity upon him when He made him after His own likeness. From the outset, therefore, the human race is special, both in God's sight and in their essential makeup. Man is a natural creature in that he is constituted of the same elements that are found in other animals. He partook of a supernatural quality when God breathed into his nostrils the breath of life. The life within him is directly related to God's will and purpose. As someone has said, "God formed man from the substance of earth and infused him with the substance of heaven." Man is the most exquisite product of God's creative genius. He was made at the very last of the creative week as the pinnacle of God's power and grace. He was the topping on creation's cake.

The psalmist grasped this truth and gloried in it. So must we if we are to properly appreciate our role in the plan of God. Man is not only a special creature but a specialized creation. God gave him powers that elevated him to a place of dominance. He is not simply a sophisticated animal; he is a person constituted in the likeness of the Divine Person.

Theodore Roosevelt was surely one of the most impressive men ever to serve as president of the United States. His dynamic personality overwhelmed those who met him. A visitor from England who came to this country during Roosevelt's administration said that the two most wonderful things he had seen in America were Niagara Falls and the president, "both great wonders of nature."

Every person, however, is a wonder. Two thousand years ago they talked about the Seven Wonders of the World. Each was very impressive, and people traveled long distances to see them. But the greatest wonder of all is a person created in the image of God. Only in the Bible are we given the understanding of man's true significance. Some Bible students have mentally exempted the early chapters of Genesis from their Bibles because of the seeming conflict with modern science. In so doing, however, they are eliminating biblical revelation of the exalted nature of man. Neither science nor any other human investigation can unveil man in his essential dignity.

The Universal Dignity of Man

The dignity of the first man and woman was passed along to succeeding generations. In Genesis 9:1, God gave instructions to Noah and the other survivors of the flood. Their commission was essentially the same as that of the first human beings. "Be fruitful, and multiply, and replenish the earth." God warned Noah and his family against human bloodshed. "Whoso sheddeth man's blood, by man shall his blood be shed: for in the image of God made he man" (v. 6) In other words, human life is sacred. It should be held in high esteem because every person is made in the image of God.

Billy Graham gave Ethel Waters a testimonial dinner several years ago. He asked the great vocal artist how she had maintained a positive outlook on life in view of the fact she was black and a female. Her reply is classic because it vividly voices the truth of Genesis. "I've lived out of the belief that God creates no inferior products." Every individual is a person of worth and value.

Genesis 5:1-3 sets forth the same principle as it speaks of the generations of Adam. There is reiterated the fact that, when God created man, He made him in His own image and likeness, both male and female. It is said that Adam fathered a son "in his own likeness, after his image." The significance of this statement is that the divine image is passed along from one generation to another. No one is left out. You and I are as much in the image of God as was the first human being.

Walking with God

In his latter years as president of Washington and Lee University, Robert E. Lee took a daily horseback ride with his daughter, Mildred. When she could not go, Lee often asked Professor White to join him. White and Lee became rather close friends. When someone asked him, however, if he had been a confidential friend of Lee he answered, "No, sir. No man was great enough to be intimate with General Lee."

Certainly no human being is inherently great enough to have fellowship with God. This is a privilege He has extended to us, one which He intended when He created us in His own image. An intimacy of relationship is suggested in the story of God visiting the garden and talking with Adam and Eve. The guilt of their disobedience interrupted this fellowship as they hid from God. God called for them, "Where art thou?" God invited fellowship and desired communication with this unique being. He had made it possible by constituting man a person in His own likeness. God and man could enjoy interpersonal association.

Fellowship with God Lends Dignity

The possibility of fellowship lends dignity to the human race. The fact that someone is a close personal friend of the president of the United States immediately gives that person status. He shares some of the aura of the White House. We are not worthy, regardless of our superior natures, to enjoy the friendship of God. But He elevates us to a place of honor when He comes calling for us. No other creature is equipped or is called to have fellowship with God.

Each human being is someone of consequence. The true merit of man can be understood and appreciated only against the backdrop of his special creation as a being capable of fellowship with God. As Christians, we view humanity in the light of God's redemptive concern as ultimately expressed in Jesus Christ. If God cares so much for us, then we must be of infinite worth. To demean the human race is to belittle God.

Humanism places the individual at the center of his world and says that he has merit as a creature of worth in his own right. There is a limited sense in which this is true. Human dignity is, indeed, reflected in such things as superior intelligence, natural abilities, and moral sensitivities. But to view the human race apart from God is to get only a partial picture. To look at man as a purely natural phenomenon is like viewing the moon with the naked eye. One can marvel at its soft, luminous beauty and wonder at its dark configurations. What a difference, however, to look at the moon with the aid of the Palomar telescope, where the mountains and the valleys and the craters loom into view. The Bible is our Palomar where the marvelous facets of human nature are revealed.

No Respecter of Persons

Since every person is of equal value in the sight of God, then inevitably a just and gracious God treats all people alike. Paul's great expression of this insight is found in Colossians 3:10-11. "And have put on the new man, which is renewed in knowledge after the image of him that created him: Where there is neither Greek nor Jew, circumcision nor uncircumcision, Barbarian, Scythian, bond nor free: but Christ is all, and in all." In other words, through Christ there is being revealed the ideal of the Creator, that all people are one before God. God doesn't favor one branch of humanity more than another. The Hebrew people were selected of God for a special purpose in His redemptive plan. They were chosen only in the sense that God called them to a mission, not that they were superior in the family of man. It has been difficult for mankind to recognize the equal merit of all peoples before God. There is a natural pride and sense of exclusiveness that clings to us and creates a clannishness that divides humanity into factions based on race, color, geography, culture, and nationalities. The tendency to look down upon others and to consider segments of humanity as inferior is completely inconsistent with the idea of all men created in the image of God.

A Lutheran minister preached a sermon on the experiences of Jonah, whom God called to preach in Nineveh. He made the point that the aim of our national political policy should be to save Russian lives as well as American. He said that with God there is "no respecter of persons" and the Ninevites were as precious to Him as the Israelites. In the congregation that day was a retired army general who said to the minister afterward, "You know, I've never quite understood it that way before. God loves the Russians as much as He does the Americans."

The barriers that divide humanity are, therefore, artificial. They are based upon superficial differences that disregard the essential unity of mankind. There is a "likeness" far greater than our differences. That likeness issues from our common origin in which God made us in His own image. The commonality of man lies much deeper than the surface disparities by which we sometimes judge each other, such as the color of the skin, the shape of the eyes, the curvature of the nose. Some of us were shortchanged when it comes to physical appearance. Pope John, sitting for his portrait, remarked, "The Good Lord knew from all eternity I would become pope. Wouldn't you think He could have made me a little more photogenic?" Fortunately, God does not look on the outward appearance in evaluating our worth. We're all precious in His sight because we reflect back to Him His own image in our totality, which, of course, includes the spirit of man.

Mutual Appreciation

Since all people are of equal dignity before God, then it naturally follows that we should treat one another with mutual respect. There are no inferior classes upon which we should look down or mistreat.

Cain complained to God that in his condition of exile he would be a fugitive and a vagabond in the earth and that everyone would abuse him. It is said that the Lord set a mark upon Cain lest anyone finding him should kill him. God cared for Cain even though he had slain his brother. There are no pariah people where God is concerned. The proper attitude of man toward his fellowman is one of appreciation and concern.

A prominent denominational leader was shocked to receive a letter from a college student who stated that he had approached the leader after a session of a recent convention, wishing to speak with him. The student said that "a friend of yours came up and you turned from me to greet him. I'm sorry that I'm a nobody, and you didn't have time to talk with me. I really needed to ask you something."

It is difficult to relate to everyone in the same congenial way. As human beings, we have natural preferences and special friendships. Nevertheless, we should always be careful to avoid creating a feeling of "nobodyism." This does a great injustice in that it denies the equal merit of every person before God.

An Expression of Irreverence

Putting down of our fellowman may be one of the greatest crimes we commit against each other as human beings. It is also one of our most irreverent expressions toward God. It is taking that which God made holy and treating it with contempt. While in Israel recently, I went through the Holocaust Museum in Jerusalem. It is a memorial to the six million Jews who died at the hands of the Nazis. Millions of others suffered great indignities and still bear not only the brand on their body but also the scars on their soul. As I saw exhibit after exhibit displaying the sadistic and cruel treatment of these unfortunate people, it seemed like some nightmare from which one awakens and finds it isn't true. I could hardly believe that a cultured and civilized nation could have so cruelly abused fellow human beings as though they were utterly without worth.

Then I remembered an occasion in which, during that same time period, a small black boy attended the daily Vacation Bible School in the country church of which I was pastor. The community became aroused, I was threatened, and some members quit coming to church. It all seemed so inconceivable that they should feel threatened and indignant over another small human being who happened to be black. We had often sung in our Sunday School, "Red and yellow, black and white, They are precious in His sight." If they are precious in God's sight, they should also be precious in our sight. God's image is found in every person on earth. This bestows upon each life a natural dignity which deserves recognition and respect.

Arthur Miller, the American playwright, made a speech a few years ago to a Congress of American Psychologists in which he said that, without human values, one cannot have good science. He told how Nazi doctors experimented with people by dropping them into a swimming pool with instruments connected to their bodies to reveal what happened when they were drowning. Previously, such studies could be made only by autopsy after the death of a drowned person. Miller declared that, on an objective basis, this might be considered an increase in knowledge, but it was not science. Afterwards, about twenty-five persons, all professional psychologists, gathered around Miller and asked, "Why isn't it science?" Miller replied, "I submit that nobody can ask that question who is not poisoned by an ideology which has within itself the possibilities of destroying the human race."[1]

Self-respect

Since I am a person made in the image of God, I should, therefore, treat myself with respect. A proper self-image is necessary for mental and spiritual health. A psychiatrist recently said that the majority of his patients were filled with self-contempt and self-hate. "They just can't stand themselves." One of the favorite pastimes of many people is to compare themselves unfavorably with others. They despise the image they see reflected in the mirror.

The Bible encourages us to love ourselves. One of two commandments Jesus quoted says, "Thou shalt love thy neighbor as thyself" (Matt. 22:39). As a matter of fact, we can hardly love our neighbor unless we love ourselves. Until we accept ourselves, we tend to rate our fellowman rather low. We're jealous, spiteful, and selfish in our

attitudes about our contemporaries. We find it difficult to say anything good about them because we don't feel good about ourselves.

A first step on the ladder out of this awful abyss of negative feelings
is the realization that God loves each of us and lovingly created each
of us in His own image. I am worthwhile because God made me that
way. There is as much of God invested in my life as that of any other
human being. Many years ago, when I took up photography as a
hobby, I learned to develop and print pictures. I enjoyed taking a
photograph of friends and making enlargements in my darkroom. I
would then proudly present them with the image of themselves. I was
dismayed when I found that most of them didn't like the picture. They
thought it was not a good likeness. We carry about in our minds a
picture of ourselves that may be very inaccurate. It is possibly too
flattering or, as is often the case, quite unbecoming. We may see
ourselves as awkward, inept, unworthy of anyone's friendship. The
Bible presents the truest likeness when it portrays us in the image of
God. There is every reason, therefore, to lift up our heads in a new
self-appreciation.

The Peril of Pride

One of the risks God took when He made man a self-aware person
was that man might be overtaken with vanity and pride. Pride is the
opposite of self-contempt. It is an inflated sense of self-worth. A
creature made in the image of God aspires to be God. "Ye shall be
as gods," was the allurement of the serpent to Eve (Gen. 3:5). Man's
basic temptation is that of making himself God. Pride, therefore, is
the primeval sin, the sin of preempting God.

The human being can become overbearing and self-important. The
Jewish Talmud asks, "Why was man created on the sixth day?" The
answer is that it was to teach man, when swollen with pride, that "a
flea preceded you in Creation."

Reinhold Neibuhr called pride the original sin. He said that man's
sin is not disobedience to a divine fiat but the idolatry of making
himself his own end. Pride brought an end to paradise. Adam and Eve
were thrust from the garden. Pride continues to bring plagues upon
humanity. Thorns and thistles are our heritage because we have

sought to make ourselves too important and God nothing. Napoleon exemplified human arrogance when he took the crown from the pope's hand and placed it upon his own head. Soon after pride's conquest in Eden, we see one human being begin to abuse another in the death of Abel at the hands of Cain. Pride fosters hostility and violence and has stained the good earth with a brother's blood. Not until human beings quit mimicking God and start worshiping Him will begin the road back to paradise. Only then will man rediscover his true dignity.

Reverence for Life

The most urgent need in the world today is the recognition of this human worth. Sometimes it appears that we place greater value on things like oil, national pride, and economic prosperity than we do upon people. Persons are expendable. It seems that we are being enveloped by a new "Ice Age." The cold is seeping through the cracks in our emotions so that we can scarcely care what happens to the rest of the human race as long as we have it good. Our city is experiencing a drought. We are prohibited from watering our lawns. With anguish, we watch our yards turn yellow and die. In the morning newspaper, there was an item about millions of people in Africa who are facing death because of a long-standing drought. This information was probably shrugged off by the majority of local readers. It is not just that we feel helpless in the face of the impending tragedy but that we have become calloused to human suffering. The continuous warfare with the loss of millions of lives has hardened us to human misery. George Sand, a novelist of the last century, told that while in Paris she took in a number of plays which accented violence. She said, "Each evening, I see an execution, a hanging, a suicide, or at least a poisoning, with the accompaniment of cries, convulsions, and death agonies. It's charming. I'm growing a bit blase, and my sensitivity has been so dulled that I laughed my head off."[2]

Growing Impersonality

The constant exposure on television and the movies to the same sort of thing in our day, I believe, tends to cultivate an indifference to the value of life. An every-evening diet in which human beings are snuffed out by the dozens creates a sentiment, What is one more life? More and more we are living an isolated existence, as we move from the warm personal relationship of the town to the cold impersonality of the city, where we seclude ourselves behind the walls of high rises. Even in our small city, we build board fences around our yards and often don't know our neighbors. A few years ago a hurricane blew down the fences, and for a brief while, we visited and shared. What kind of a hurricane will it take to tear down the fences of unconcern that segregate us on our separate icebergs?

For those who view man in the biblical context as created in the image of God, many violations of the reverence for life can be seen in our social order today. The human being as the crown of God's creation and constituted in the image of God must be handled with caution. One must not be callously exploited or carelessly disposed of. Every human life is a treasure to be cherished, an awesome marvel of God's grace and power. In life and in death, one should be accorded respect.

Nuclear War

The use of nuclear weapons in international conflict is at least an option today. More and more nations are acquiring nuclear missiles and other devices. It seems inconceivable that, in some future war, these mighty weapons would not be used. George Bernard Shaw said that man has not invented a weapon which he has not used. I can't evaluate that statement, but I fear that nuclear warheads will be employed. This is one reason the human race cannot afford to consider war. The inevitable devastation makes it impractical. Who would survive to gloat over the victory?

The newspaper reported recently that nineteen Nobel Prize scientists and 178 leaders of environmental and arms reduction groups have been meeting to discuss the fate of humanity. They issued the statement that, unless humanity changes its ways, mankind faces extinction, either through a nuclear war or an environmental catastrophe. Even a limited nuclear war, they said, could produce enough smoke and soot to block out nearly all of the Northern Hemisphere's sunlight, plunging the planet for many months into a dark, lethal, nuclear winter. The fact that human life would be sacrificed on such an enormous scale makes consideration of nuclear war sheer madness. Each Poseidon submarine has 10 missiles, each of which has 14 MIRV warheads, each of which is equivalent to the Hiroshima bomb. Every submarine carries enough power to destroy 140 Hiroshimas. The 11,000 nuclear warheads America possesses could destroy the world population twelves times over. A document entitled "The Effects of Nuclear War" put out by the U. S. Congress suggests a hypothetical situation in which the U.S.S.R. struck first and the U. S. retaliated. A very large attack could destroy up to 77 percent of the American people and up to 40 percent of the Russians. Many millions more would die later of injuries or starve or freeze to death the following winter.[3]

It is an act of disrespect on a grand scale that human beings would create such hideous weapons with the potential of human decimation. We are standing on a perilous brink when, by the pushing of a few buttons, mankind can largely destroy that which God created as the ultimate expression of His divine forethought. God alone has the right to destroy the human race, and He decided after the Flood not to exercise that prerogative again. People are too wonderful to turn into the debris of nuclear war.

The proper ethical stance in view of the sacredness of life is for nations and individuals to work as hard for peace as they do for war, to hallow human life as something too precious to sacrifice on the altar of hostility and disrespect.

Capital Punishment

Another issue which must be considered in the light of the reverence for life is capital punishment. The taking of a human life under whatever circumstances is a serious matter. There have been times in history when life or death rested upon the whim of a tyrant. A classic illustration was the crucifixion of Jesus, when the clamor of a mob, rather than justice, was the deciding factor. The beheading of John the Baptist at the behest of a dancing girl and her spiteful mother is another example. While there is no doubt that certain crimes deserve the severest punishment, often history bears sordid record to the willy-nilly destruction of life by those in authority in a wanton exercise of power. In the year 1800 there were 223 offenses punishable by death in Great Britain.

Billy Graham expressed a reluctance about capital punishment in an interview. "We live in a time of horrible and hideous crimes. But one of the hesitations I've had is that so many more black people are executed. The system has always been too one-sided, and many of the people on death row are poor people who couldn't afford good lawyers."[4]

Human justice must always be fallible. In view of this, capital punishment, if done at all, should be carried out only after the most careful investigation and deliberation. A human life is at stake, and the action can never be reversed.

Jails and Prisons

It is not only in the death sentence, however, that human dignity is sometimes violated. Information is being published about the inhuman conditions and treatment in jails and prisons. A federal judge said recently that hundreds of grown men are being held in custody for as much as twenty-three hours per day in less space than is required by law for a dog or cat. He was criticizing a Midwestern prison where conditions, he felt, violated the United States Constitution. What about violating the basic dignity of man as created in the image of God? The conditions in many prisons foster violence and confirm prisoners in a life of crime. The F.B.I. reports that 74 percent of those released from prison are rearrested within four years. The prisons apparently do not just punish criminals; they make criminals.

Charles Colson, who spent time in prison for Watergate crimes and now has a Christian ministry to prisoners, says, "The whole system of punishment today is geared toward taking away people's dignity." He declares that prisons are overcrowded, understaffed, dirty places. "Eighty percent of American prisons are barbaric." We must find ways of dealing with criminals as persons created in the image of God.

Abortion

In January 1973 the Supreme Court ruled that state laws unduly restricting the right to abortion were unconstitutional. Since then there has been an enormous increase in abortions. A strong movement called "Right to Life" has stoutly opposed abortions, insisting that the fetus is a person with a fundamental right to be born. On the other hand, the women's liberation movement has proclaimed the right of a woman to exercise her own judgment in how she uses her body. People are caught in the vortex of conflicting opinions which are being expressed with great emotion and conviction.

Hardly anyone believes that abortion should never be considered under any circumstances. Even most opponents to abortion make allowances for it when the life of the mother is at stake or in the case of incest and rape. Most abortions are not performed under these circumstances or sought for medical reasons. Social and economic circumstances that have to do with the woman's life situation constitute the basis for the majority of cases.

The Bible does not have any direct teaching on the subject of abortion. By inference, however, there is a certain moral consideration for the Christian. Since we believe that human life has a special sanctity, it cannot be disposed of without valid ethical considerations. This would, presumably, apply to the unborn child as a human entity in potential, if not in reality. There is a great debate among physicians, theologians, and politicians as to when the fetus becomes a person. Some say at the moment of conception life is begun and must be dealt with responsibly. The Supreme Court divided gestation into three trimesters of twelve weeks each. During the first trimester the decision is left completely in the hands of the doctor and patient. The state would not interfere.

During the second trimester, the state could regulate the extent to which the laws related to the "preservation and protection of maternal health." In other words, from the fourth to the sixth month, the woman may be required to have her abortion at an approved hospital by a licensed physician. During the third trimester, the state can prohibit abortion except when necessary to save the mother's health.[5]

Several denominations have gone on record as opposing abortion on demand. However, while basically opposed to abortion, the door is usually left open for abortion as an acceptable recourse under very special circumstances. This seems to reflect the opinion of most Christians and is consistent with the dignity of human life.

Pornography

What is pornography? It is anything that deals with human sexuality in an ugly and demeaning fashion. When sin entered the picture, Adam and Eve became painfully aware of their nakedness. Pornography is associated with human depravity. The soiled mind of man takes something beautiful and makes it dirty. Sexuality is a divine gift meant for holy purposes. Pornography makes smutty that which God made sacred. It degrades the human race to a bestial level.

Man was made for high thoughts, noble actions, and compassionate personal relationships. These things are consistent with his creation in the image of God. Obscenity attacks the moral citadel of humanity. It drags minds from the clouds into the gutter; it encourages the kind of shameful behavior that is irresponsible and earthy. It creates a selfish, lustful spirit in association with others in which they are treated as things rather than persons.

The courts have found it difficult to define pornography. This is true, in part, because of the differing viewpoints among people. What to one person may seem evil to another may appear normal. There is a sense in which obscenity is relative.

Regardless of the problem in defining pornography, each of us can probably pinpoint those influences which are detrimental to our spiritual well-being. The law has become careless in defending our country against this moral enemy. Attitudes, generally, have become complacent. This does not mean that pornography has suddenly become innocent.

Recently, the first black Miss America was relieved of her crown because a magazine presented nude and erotic pictures of her made prior to her winning the contest. The publisher of the magazine defended his actions by saying there was nothing wrong with the pictures.

View of Womanhood

While pornography is one of the most prevalent ways of demeaning womanhood, there is a general attitude about women that considers them second class. Aristotle, long ago, declared that women are inferior to men. If Aristotle said it, the ancient world was inclined to accept it.

The creation story speaks of Eve as a helpmate but says nothing about the relative merit of Adam and Eve. In fact, the Bible says that man was created male and female and both were in the image of God, the woman no less than the man (Gen. 1:26-27). Therefore, to treat women as inferior or to assign them a secondary role is to deny the divine endowment equally distributed to the whole of humanity.

In many ways, it would seem that the shoe is on the other foot when it comes to determining relative merit. Women outlive men on the average of eight years. They usually make better grades in school. They often have superior dexterity. More women than men attend church, which indicates a spiritual superiority. They have more social graces and can endure more pain. I'm afraid that the lack of equality is a male invention rather than a biblical revelation.

Miscellaneous Indignities

This chapter could go on and on because our social order is packed with examples of ways in which we do ill service to the dignity of the human race. The exploitation of people in the labor market is one of the most damaging. When a person is not properly paid for the work he does, it injures his own sense of self-worth and expresses the lack of appreciation on the part of the employer. Jesus expressed the principle in these words, "The laborer is worthy of his hire" (Luke 10:7). Cheap labor cheapens laborers. Women are, of course, among the most poorly recompensed people in our society. This again reflects the inferior status to which they are often assigned. A wholesome recognition of human dignity is afforded through adequate appreciation and compensation for one's labor.

In the book, *The Windsor Story,* the author says that the most enduring grievance on the part of the Duke of Windsor's staff was the fact that the Windsors never expressed a compliment for any staff service. A woman who had worked for them for ten years said that it was impossible for either the duke or the duchess to express appreciation. The servants were made to feel dispensable and that the Windsors were doing them an honor by their employment. If that were the case, then the servants became things to the Windsors, rather than valued persons. This illustration forcefully brings to mind the importance of treating each individual, whether the maid in the home, the yardman, secretary, or shift worker, with respect and consideration in keeping with their divine dignity.

George Bernard Shaw's secretary was being complimented upon her splendid privilege of working for the literary giant. She paused and then said, "It would have been even more splendid if just once in the forty years, he had said thank you."

The starving millions in the Third World countries test our sense of human worth. Can those who have plenty ignore the plight of those who never know what it is to have enough of life's essentials? Humanitarian appeals often fall on deaf ears because of the remoteness of these suffering people from our affluent world and, also, because our overstuffed society is selfishly satisfied to enjoy our prosperity. This casual attitude places a great host of humanity on the level of insects whose demise makes little difference. Our interest level in the needs of our fellowman quickly displays our feelings about the value of life.

There is a current trend toward quick and cheap disposal of the human body after death. Books have been written criticizing the cosmetic craft of the funeral industry and the economic gouging of relatives in the emphasis upon expensive burials. While some of the accusations may be accurate, the impression is left that the body is of little value once the spirit has departed. Therefore, it makes little difference what is done with the corpse. As we have observed in a previous chapter, the entire person, body and spirit, was created in the image of God. In keeping, therefore, with this inherent dignity, the body should be disposed of with respect.

People are precious. Like valuable packages, they should be handled with care.

Notes

1. Arthur Miller, "The Role of P.E.N.," *The Saturday Review,* June 4, 1966, p. 17.

2. Curtis, Cate, *George Sand* (Boston: Houghton, Mifflin & Co., 1955, p. 155.

3. "Calling for Peacemakers in a Nuclear Age," Part 1, *Christianity Today,* February 8, 1980, p. 44.

4. *The Progressives,* August, 1982, p. 28.

5. James D. Pleitz, "An Abortion Primer," *Search,* February, 1975, p. 25.

7
Male and Female

Male-Female Tension

A teenage girl was discussing marriage with her mother. The daughter expressed the opinion that it was a fine thing for a man and woman who were different in personality, background, tastes, and the like to marry because they tend to complement each other. The mother wisely remarked, "Just being man and woman is difference enough."

It was good that God differentiated the human race into two sexes, male and female, but He also set the stage for deep-seated tensions that have persisted across the ages. The movement of women for equal rights is an indication that, while men and women need each other, they also have difficulty in relating to each other. There are inherent differences which create a gap which both find difficult to cross.

Someone has illustrated the sexual conflict by calling attention to the way in which words and phrases are often slanted in the favor of the man. For example, an unmarried man is a "bachelor," while the single woman is an "old maid." What he hears at the office is "news"; what she hears at the bridge party is "gossip." When he is in command of the family, he is the "head of the house." When she is assertive, she "wears the pants in the family." His gray hair gives him a distinguished look but makes her appear old. In a man's world, the woman is often the target of the big put-down.

Nothing is said in the creation story to indicate dominance or superiority of one sex over another. The woman is not portrayed as occupying a secondary role, which is sometimes assumed because she was created after Adam (Gen. 2). Genesis 1:27, however, belies this idea. "So God created man in his own image, in the image of God created he him; male and female, created he them." I conceive of God creating mankind as a unit. The creation of woman was not an afterthought. The duality of humankind was God's intent from the outset.

The Same but Different

Men and women are the same species. They are equally man. The Hebrew word for *man* in the generic sense is *adam*. It is found 562 times in the Old Testament and is used predominantly to mean mankind or humankind in general, which includes both male and female. Men and women are equally in the image of God; therefore, they share in equal dignity. Dominion belongs to both, as described in Genesis 1:26: "Let *them* have dominion over the fish of the sea" (author's italics). "Them" refers to the whole human race. No attempt is made in the creation story to set up the male as a superior human with the female tagging along for the benefit of the male. They are partners, sharing the same uniqueness and dignity.

With humans, just as in the rest of the animal kingdom, God established a male-female differentiation. When God presented to Adam his helpmate, I am sure that Adam immediately noticed the difference. This distinction between the sexes is indicated in Genesis 2:23, where the word for *man* is *ish* rather than *adam*. The female form is *ishah*. These words are employed when a sexual identity is being made in referring to humanity. *Ish* and *ishah* are human counterparts, each serving a needed and distinctive function in their shared existence.

Equal but Unequal

It is often assumed that the male is biologically superior because he is usually larger and stronger than the female. Such a conclusion is difficult to sustain in view of the longer life expectancy of the woman. While 125 males are conceived for every 100 females, the proportion of males born alive is much less. The U. S. Census lists 64 specific causes of death, and in 57 of these, females show a lower rate than males. Women seem to be naturally endowed with a greater physical durability than men.

Made for Companionship.

"It is not good that the man should be alone" (Gen. 2:18). These words reflect God's sensitiveness to man's need of human association. God had provided the other animals with companions of their own kind, but Adam was alone in the world. No one could understand his needs or share his responsibilities.

Sentimentally and sexually, we are created with the possibility and the instinct for companionship. Loneliness, no doubt, is one of the greatest burdens that some people have to bear. This is especially true in the case of those who have forfeited companions through divorce or death. Life loses much of its incentive and purpose when people are lonely. Human beings need socialability not solitude. Being alone is a helpless feeling (Eccl. 4:9-11).

Our churches today have become more aware of the plight of singles. Contact with other persons is one of the most urgent needs of this group. God's creative purpose was that man should live in association rather than isolation. John Donne was to the point when he said, "No man is an island." Living without human relationships is an abnormal situation.

God provided a partner.—God alone could provide a partner for the first man. God said, "I will make him an help meet for him" (Gen. 2:18). Man could not be human alone; the animals could not relate to man; man needed a person like himself. There is a suggestive symbolism in God making woman from the side of man. Perhaps it indicates an initial bonding so that man would not feel content without woman and woman, not satisfied without man. A deep relationship would develop as each found his sexual counterpart and formed a family.

Beyond sexuality.—The attraction between the sexes is basically biological but goes much deeper than that. The words "help meet for him" express the intent of God. The phrase literally means "a helper to meet him face to face." This other person was one with whom he could enter into responsible relations. They were to be companions and share life's responsibilities. This was a setting in which romance and love could transpire. Each person needs someone who deeply cares for him, with whom he can share both the burdens and the intimacies of life. Sexuality plays a vital role in this relationship, but human companionship is not just for the purpose of gratifying physical urges. Man as a person needs other persons, especially one other person to whom he can relate in an exclusive and satisfying companionship.

Men and women in this kind of a partnership are communicating on a level possible only to creatures made in the image of God. God constituted man with a capacity of forming a gratifying identity with another person. This is a reflection of the interpersonal relationships in the Godhead: God the Father, Son, and Holy Spirit. Needs of affection, support, encouragement, and friendship are met. Not just a physical but also a spiritual bonding takes place.

The Case for Monogamy

Many people today think monogamy is equal to monotony. The number of couples living together without any binding commitment is on the increase. The divorce rate almost matches the number of marriages. The youth of our nation are being conditioned to look upon marriage as either undesirable or tentative. Multiple relationships are said to be more natural than exclusive associations with one person. Biblical ideals are being abandoned. In this context, Christians need to uphold the intent of God in providing for the marriage of a man and woman in a lasting relationship.

The Desirability of the Woman

Genesis 2:24 speaks of the man leaving his father and mother and cleaving to his wife. Such words imply the attractiveness of the woman to the man. She is so desirable that he is willing to leave his parents and his childhood home to live with her. He experiences a strong appeal to his physical and emotional nature. The words, also, indicate a natural inclination to focus his desire upon one woman who becomes his loving companion. Monogamy is, therefore, structured into the divine ideal.

God's Design for Marriage

The words "cleave unto his wife" suggest both the sexual aspect of marriage and the enduring nature of the union. Cleaving to his wife is contrasted with the leaving of his parents. The two become one flesh, suggesting the permanent nature of the relationship. There is an amalgamation both of bodies and of souls. In this new dynamic union, the man and the woman discover their full personhood. The later Scriptures also magnify the enduring nature of marriage in the application of this passage. Jesus quoted the words as a reinforcement of his teaching about marriage and divorce. "Have ye not read, that he which made them at the beginning made them male and female, And said, For this cause shall a man leave father and mother, and shall cleave to his wife: and they twain shall be one flesh? Wherefore they are no more twain, but one flesh" (Matt. 19:4-6).

Monogamy was not an invention of man but inherent in his social structure. One man and one woman for a lifetime was God's design for marriage from the beginning. This principle has been violated, denied, and ignored, but it is still the avenue to life's richest human experiences for those who choose to marry.

Chastity

Faithfulness to the marriage union is also intimated in the expression, "cleave to his wife." Previous generations of man lived by a double standard in which the woman was expected to be pure and loyal to her husband, but the man was often regarded in a different light. He was simply being a "man" when he went on the prowl. In fact, the unfaithful husband is acting more on the beastly level. By creative design, both partners to the marriage have a responsibility to be true. They are to cleave to each other.

Love and Sex

Nothing is said in the Genesis account about love, but God well knew that love would flourish in this union. Created in the image of God, men and women were uniquely endowed with a capacity for affection since love is the predominant characteristic of God. Love cannot exist unless it has an object. I suspect that, in the instance of Adam and Eve, it was a case of love at first sight. I also suspect that the sexual relationship awaited their growing intimacy and increasing love for each other.

A relationship that is purely for sexual pleasure violates the intent of God. There is no place in the creation story for sex as a fun-and-games sort of thing. It is reserved for the leaving and cleaving experience in which a man and woman, by mutual choice, enter into a loving and enduring union.

A middle-aged woman, commenting on the joys of marriage, said, "I'm glad I have this man to love." She did not say, "a man," but, "this man." The focus of her love is a particular man with a particular name and personality. The years together had not diminished the thrill of her loving or the joy of her being with this man. Outside the marriage setting of a love relationship, sex can become boring and uneventful. In a tender and enduring companionship, it is enhanced and enriched as the years go by. This is the way God meant it to be.

Nudity and Crudity

"And they were both naked, the man and his wife, and were not ashamed" (Gen. 2:25). Marriage is a context in which nudity is natural and unshameful. The Lord did an outstanding construction job when He made the human form. God intended that men and women should be attractive to each other as an encouragement to mating and the development of family life. What God has made should never be considered vulgar in its proper place. The bodies of the husband and wife are for each other's appreciation and enjoyment. Unfortunately, the display of the body has become commercialized. This is like forcing a jewel out of its setting. The entertainment industry more and more utilizes nudity as a means of attracting audiences. Bare beaches flourish in some areas. That which God intended to be reserved for the privacy of marriage companions is being publicly exhibited for the titillation of strangers. This can only cheapen that which God gave us as a treasure to be cherished between lifetime partners.

The ancient world worshiped sex in the form of idols with exaggerated sexual features. We are approaching that kind of paganism today when we idolize persons with extraordinary sexual endowments. Their images appear on posters, magazine covers, and billboards portrayed in the most lurid ways possible. The nude form is not shameful but has been exploited in shameful ways that tend to demoralize society and project sexuality in an unwholesome light.

The Precious Intimacy

"And they shall be one flesh" (Gen. 2:24). Marriage is an amalgamation of lives, not just a togetherness. Jesus said, "And they twain shall be one flesh" (Matt. 19:5). This truth is symbolized in the sexual union. The blending of lives, however, goes beyond the mere joining of bodies. It is the sharing of selves. There transpires a spiritual, psychological, and emotional identification. Someone has poetically said that, though they walk together, they leave only one set of prints. Their thoughts, desires, feelings, and goals are intermingled, and they move together as a unit. This is something that can transpire only in a one-to-one relationship bonded in love. Marriage is a partnership so intimate that the partners have become one larger and more complete self. The richest and sweetest experiences of life are discovered in this oneness.

Theodore Roosevelt wrote a letter to his niece, Eleanor, when the announcement was made of her engagement to Franklin Roosevelt. His words constitute a beautiful and accurate assessment of marriage. "Married life has many cares and trials; but it is only in the married life that the highest and finest happiness is to be found." He then wrote to Franklin, "No other success in life—not the presidency, or anything else—begins to compare with the joy and happiness that come in and from the love of the true man and the true woman."[1]

Marriage in the real sense is not a formality, a liaison between a man and a woman for the convenience of sex or whatever. It is a friendship on the deepest level of love in which two people are not merely husband and wife. They are two individuals who have been joined together in one unit of personal intimacy in which neither loses his own personhood but together gains a new and satisfying identity.

Sexuality and Parenthood

Human sexuality is a gratifying experience for the bonded lovers but has as its basic purpose the procreation of the species. This, too, is a joyous consequence of sexual mating. In Genesis 4:1 we read, "And Adam knew Eve his wife; and she conceived, and bare Cain, and said, I have gotten a man from the Lord." God is the Creator; man is the procreator. In this sense, he is cooperating with God in perpetuating the race and helping to realize the creative design that the earth should always have a human caretaker. The deep-seated sexual impulse guarantees the continuity of humanity.

The producing of children gives a sacred significance to the sexual union. It is an awesome responsibility to bring into being a new generation. Parents assume an enormous obligation to carefully and lovingly rear the child in a way that he or she can achieve full maturity and become a responsible person.

Through the reproductive process, the image of God is passed along in the lifestream of humanity. Genesis 5:3 says, "And Adam lived a hundred and thirty years, and begat a son in his own likeness, after his image." Human beings give birth to other human beings who inherit the image in which God created that first person. Personhood is perpetuated through the procreative union. Thus, each human being who ever lived can be said to be in the image of God.

Sexuality and Family Planning

Some Christian groups strongly insist that the sexual union between husbands and wives is exclusively for procreation. They say that every intimacy must have the possibility of impregnation. This interpretation precludes the use of contraceptives as a means of preventing unwanted pregnancies. Those who espouse this view experience a burden of guilt when they engage in sex purely for pleasure. Couples, also, experience a sexual strain if they deny themselves these intimacies for fear of having children. Furthermore, many families produce more children than they can properly provide for. This concept is one of the contributing factors to world overpopulation.

People do not have sexual seasons like animals which mate for reproduction. This would imply, therefore, that human sexuality must have some additional purpose than childbearing. In the first one hundred thirty years of Adam and Eve's marriage, it hardly seems likely that they "knew" each other only a few times. In those years, we are told they had three children. In that case, it would have been a very abstemious marriage, or they would have had more children. Such rare sexual intercourse would have been a very unnatural circumstance.

Paul realized that sexual activity for husbands and wives was desirable and proper.

> The husband should fulfill his marital duty to his wife, and likewise the wife to her husband. The wife's body does not belong to her alone but also to her husband. In the same way, the husband's body does not belong to him alone but also to his wife. Do not deprive each other except by mutual consent and for a time, so that you may devote yourselves to prayer. Then come together again so that Satan will not tempt you because of your lack of self-control (1 Cor. 7:3-5, NIV).

The biblical word for the sexual experience is "to know." "Adam knew Eve his wife" (Gen. 4:1). The word obviously means experiential knowledge rather than simply intellectual. Adam and Eve experienced each other at the greatest depth of interpersonal relationship. They realized to the full extent the physical and emotional unity anticipated in their creative design as male and female. The sexual encounter between marriage partners is a fulfilling and satisfying experience in which they discover dimensions of themselves otherwise undisclosed. This intimacy seals their bond and contributes immeasurably to their sense of nearness and dearness. God must have had this in mind when He made mankind with specialized sexual instincts and possibilities.

Sexuality and Celibacy

The idea that celibacy, or the single life entirely devoid of any sexual union, made a person spiritually superior developed in the early church. A cult developed about the virgin Mary which idealized her as the perpetual virgin, this in spite of the fact that the Bible says she bore other children in addition to Jesus. In Mark 6:3 we read, "Is not this the carpenter, the son of Mary, the brother of James, and Joses, and of Judas and Simon? and are not his sisters here with us?" Interpreters who wanted to believe that Mary never had any sexual experience said that these children were cousins of Jesus, children of Mary's sister, whose name was also Mary.

This viewpoint reflected the reluctance to accept the wholesomeness of the sexual relationship between husband and wife. Sexuality has been seen as a spiritual detriment and a concession to man's carnal nature. Since some people feel that sex taints the human spirit, they would congratulate the person who has the gift of self-denial and would consider that person to be living in closer communion with God. From this distorted attitude arose the celibate clergy.

The biblical undergirding for celibacy is found in the writings of Paul who, apparently, never married. He encouraged his readers to remain single if that were their gift. On the other hand, he said that if celibacy created an intolerable problem for them, they should marry. "It is better to marry than to burn" (1 Cor. 7:9). Paul meant that it is better to marry than to burn with sexual desire. He conceded that not every one has the gift of singlehood. He seems to disparage marriage when he said, "But and if thou marry, thou hast not sinned; and if a virgin marry, she has not sinned. Nevertheless, such shall have trouble in the flesh" (v. 28). Marriage complicates life, Paul was explaining. Paul's remarks must be interpreted in view of his belief that Christ was returning soon. He said, "The time is short" (v. 29). Marriage could distract a Christian from concentration upon his spiritual welfare in preparation for Christ's coming.

God designed man as male and female with the intent they should be joined together as mutual helpers. They should "cleave" to each other in the exclusive sexual union, the natural product of such union being that of children. There is no real biblical basis for celebrating celibacy. Neither is there a condemnation of single life if that is one's circumstance by lack of finding a suitable partner or by personal choice, as long as such persons do not violate the biblical ideal of sexual expression in the marriage context.

Faithfulness to the Sexual Union

The "one flesh" concept of marriage as revealed in Genesis 2:24 speaks strongly to the importance of fidelity in the union. The biblical ideal is that of sexual association between one man and one woman for a lifetime. No other sexual liaison is considered appropriate. To depart from this teaching violates the "one flesh" relationship. Exclusiveness is breached, and grave damage is done to the union. Some of the deepest hurts and disappointments in life are experienced through the unfaithfulness of the marriage partner. The famous mystery writer Agatha Christie suffered such a dagger wound. She then became frightened of marriage. She wrote, "I realized that the only person who can really hurt you in life is a husband. Nobody else is close enough. On nobody are you so dependent for the everyday companionship, affection, and all else that makes up marriage."[2]

Sexual infidelity leaves a fractured self on the part of both the unfaithful partner and his or her spouse. It divides that which "God hath joined." Although the marriage may survive, still there is a lingering scar. The relationship can never be what God meant it to be, a perfect oneness in heart, soul, and body.

Homosexuality

Homosexuality, sex relations between those of the same sex, is openly defended as a legitimate life-style today. It is advocated simply as a matter of sexual preference. Homosexual church congregations are being served by homosexual ministers. Denominational bodies are arguing over the recognition of these clergy and congregations. The entertainment industry is producing films and plays which portray homosexuality in a favorable light. Laws are being passed to protect such persons in the labor market. The formerly covert way of life has come to the surface in a manner that challenges old concepts.

The reading of the creation story leaves no doubt that God made two sexes and intended that sexuality should be expressed in relationship with another person of the opposite sex. The very physical makeup of an individual anticipates another person with a complementary biological build.

Homosexuality also places the sexual expression on a level of physical gratification, whereas God designed it as a means of procreating the race. Homosexuality is an aberration and a distortion of the divine intent. It is a misuse of sex for selfish purposes. Paul discussed this problem, which he found so prevalent in the Roman world:

> Because of this, God gave them over to shameful lusts. Even their women exchanged natural relations for unnatural ones. In the same way the men also abandoned natural relations with women and were inflamed with lust for one another. Men committed indecent acts with other men and received in themselves the due penalty for their perversion (Rom. 1:26-27, NIV).

A Wholesome Attitude

Because of the terribly wicked conditions of society, the early Christians tended to react negatively toward sexuality. Some saw it as the pathway to impurity and the epitome of evil. The tendency arose, therefore, to downplay sex as a part of the divine program for man. While sexuality has its temptations, this diversity of the human race into male and female is a thing to celebrate. Out of it flows such blessings as companionship, romance, helpfulness, children, and love in the most meaningful human experience.

Notes

1. Joseph P. Lash, *Eleanor and Franklin* (New York: W. W. Norton and Co., Inc., 1971), p. 138.
2. Agatha Christie, *An Autobiography* (New York: Dodd, Mead, and Co., 1977), p. 396.

8
Human Society

"And the Lord God said, It is not good that the man should be alone" (Gen. 2:18). One lone person set down in the midst of God's vast creation was not His intent. It would have been a cold and cruel Creator who would have made just one human being, who really had nothing in common with the other creatures. God, therefore, created male and female to complete the human race in potential by providing Adam a companion of the same kind but of another gender. "Male and female created he them" (Gen. 1:27). Thus, from the outset human life was established in a social setting.

Rooted in the Nature of God

God Himself exists in a kind of society, or at least in relationships within the Godhead: God the Father, the Son, and the Holy Spirit. This may be implied when God speaks of Himself in the plural: "Let us make man." There is both unity and diversity in the divine Being. He is Three in One; thus, we speak of the Holy Trinity. Man created in the image of God is a unit in that his individuality is complete, but there's a sense in which his personhood is not fully realized until he is in association with other human beings.

Created for Partnership

God is not understood unless He is seen in fellowship within His own Person. The deity of Christ is denied by those who do not grasp this significant biblical revelation. Relationship is inherent in God's nature, and man created in the image of God was made for relationship. Just as there is a unity in the Godhead, so man exists in a unitary

121

association. We are not like grains of sand on the beach, but we are a family. We are made for one another. Though we are individually distinct in sex, race, and personality, still we are one people who desperately need to be in touch with each other. Personhood is experienced only when we are in communion with other persons. Personality belongs to man alone and is the binding force in human society.

Apart from their encounter with each other, Adam and Eve's primary social outreach was with God Himself. The constitution of human life in His own image allowed for such fellowship. The human person can communicate with the Divine Person. Here lies the basis of our religious venture. God is not some far-off, distant, and impersonal Spirit but a Person who desires a relationship with the persons whom He created in His own image. Fellowship with God is surely the highest and most exciting expression of our personhood.

Human Nature Confirms

Man was made for society. This is his natural environment. Just as fish belong to the water and birds to the air, the endowments of the human race indicate that they are made for social interaction. Man's physical, emotional, and intellectual equipment suppose other persons. His capacity to speak, for example, would be to no purpose where there are not those who could be addressed and who would be able to respond. His sexuality, also, implied the existence of someone else who has sexual features that complement his own. The capacity for love would be entirely superfluous if there were no love object. As in the instance of God, this love is an outreach of one self to another self.

No Man an Island

John Donne's insight into this truth was expressed in a picturesque way. "No man is an island entire of itself; for he belongs to the great continent, a part of the main, . . . and therefore never send to know for whom the bell tolls; it tolls for thee." As the Old Testament says, we are knit together "in the bundle of life" (1 Sam. 25:29).

The very nature of each individual is to live in community with other persons. Robinson Crusoe, living alone on his island, cut off from all human association, experienced a shattering loss of personhood. There was no one to talk to, no one to share with, and no one to care. It was a grand reunion with himself when Friday appeared on the scene, and he knew once more the feeling of community. In one of his Antarctic adventures, Admiral Byrd spent the six months of the polar night alone in a tiny hut. He had brought books and a phonograph. During those lonely months in which he almost died from asphyxiation and cold, his thoughts were consumed with his family and friends. He found that these relationships mean more than anything else in life.

One of the most pathetic confessions of an empty self was penned by H. G. Wells, the imaginative author, before he died. "I am tired, I am old, I am ill. I have no gang, I have no party. My epitaph will be, 'He was clever, but not clever enough.' "[1] He was not clever enough to realize that he could not really live without a circle of loving friends. The psalmist echoed that cry of despair, "No man cared for my soul" (Ps. 142:4).

A Condition of Maturity

Each of us needs human company if we are to grow up as persons. We become aware of our own personhood only as we relate to others physically, emotionally, intellectually, and spiritually. Man is not a solitary animal. His humanity is discovered and developed through association with other human beings. One of the most popular stories of modern times is that of Tarzan, who was reared in the society of apes. His manhood remained stunted and unfulfilled until he met Jane and was introduced into the human arena. There was awakened his latent human qualities.

In my hometown, a man lived a hermit's existence. He was seldom seen outside his house, which was surrounded by dense and untended foliage. He had retreated from his personhood and, in turn, experienced the diminishment of many personality traits that marked him a human.

A great deal of emphasis is being placed today upon staying young. As a matter of fact, more attention should be given to growing up. In the effort to stay young, some people became narcissistic. That is, they became too enamored of themselves. Their concern is focused on how they look, how trim their bodies are, and how agile they are on the tennis court or golf course. Consequently, they remain perennial adolescents.

Maturity comes in cultivating an interpersonal association rather than physical calisthenics. An undue absorption in concern for oneself can be very unhealthy. It is thwarting the first demand of personhood, that of reaching out to others and learning to relate to our fellow human beings in an acceptable and creative way.

The Peril of Loneliness

Probably one of the most serious social problems today is loneliness. Millions of people live limited lives. They have fears, anxieties, and longings that harass them. In some instances, they seem to be going through the motions of life but without any real purpose. Other millions have never learned to relate and so retreat into their cocoon, peering out at the world going by. Psychologist James L. Lynch says that loneliness kills. He maintains that social isolation brings emotional and then physical deterioration. He has written that there is a biological basis for our need to form human relationships and that, if we fail to do so, our health is in peril. Poet W. H. Auden warned, "We must love one another or die."

These words simply reinforce the fact that people need people. There is an inherent and God-given instinct for association with other persons, and if it is thwarted, we endanger our health as well as inhibiting our personal development. Personal relationships cannot be neglected without consequences. We cannot find life at its best in isolation. It behooves us to take an initiative in developing meaningful contacts with our fellow human beings.

Laughing and Crying

A peculiarity of human life is the ability to express emotion through laughing and crying. No other animal is gifted with this facility in expressing feelings. Someone has pointed out that only human beings can manage the coordinated contractions of some fifteen facial muscles accompanied by an altered state of breathing we call laughter. Laughter is a social facilitator. Through it, people share their feelings of joy and exhilaration. When they can laugh together, they ease tensions, let down barriers, and form bonds that are mutually satisfying. Each public speaker knows that one way of getting a sympathetic hearing is by making the audience laugh. Laughter is a social catalyst and surely designed of God to foster friendships and help create an openness in society.

Tears are also unique to human life. There are tears of joy and tears of sorrow. Tears are an effective communication in interpersonal relationships. The hymn, "Blest Be the Tie," speaks of shedding the sympathetic tear. We can cry over each other and for each other. Many a friendship has been sealed with tears. Charles Allen tells of a little girl who went on an errand for her mother. When she was tardy in returning, her mother asked for an explanation. The child explained that a playmate down the street had fallen and broken her doll. "I stopped to help her," explained the daughter. The mother wondered what in the world her child could have done to help mend the broken doll. Her daughter gave the marvelous reply, "I just sat down and helped her cry."

Laughter and tears are both instruments of social intercourse and, no doubt, reflect the divine image in man. They hark back to the Originator, who is a God who rejoices and a God who grieves. He gifted the human being with those two qualities in such an unusual way because He wants people to dwell together in a happy and caring communion.

Playing and Working

Play Helps Create Good Social Relationships

The Olympic Games that were held in Los Angeles kept millions of us glued to our television sets for a week. We watched the athletes from over the world competing for the medals. The modern Olympics gets its tradition from those games in ancient Greece. The games were reinstated in 1896 in Athens. A French nobleman named Coubertin felt it would be good for the spirit of the times and help bring the nations together. He agitated for several years before he saw his dream fulfilled in a new marble stadium in Athens.

Play is a social expression that helps create good relationships. As long as people can play together, they can work out differences and produce an atmosphere of congeniality. Play is one of the earliest expressions of sociality. When children get together, they soon find a game to play. This instinct to play carries over into adulthood and is the stimulus for forming teams, parties, and friendships. The natural spirit of aggression and competition can be released in a harmless setting. People are brought out of themselves through participation. Often they can become a part of a group which gives them a feeling of identity with other people.

Work as a Social Agent

Through the creation story, we learn that God is industrious. Six days He labored, and on the seventh day He rested. When God made man, He shared with him the work instinct. He gave to him a task, that of caretaker for the garden of Eden. Paradise was not simply lounging around but assuming a worthwhile responsibility. The human being is divinely programmed to use his energy and talent in creative ways. The real joys of life are not found in idleness but in a useful work. Thomas Carlyle once wrote, "Blessed is he who has found his work; let him ask no other blessedness."

The work assignment from God was a joint responsibility. Before God particularized about the care of the garden, He gave Adam and Eve a broad interpretation of their mutual role. In Genesis 1:28, God said to them, "Be fruitful, and multiply, and replenish the earth, and subdue it: and have dominion over the fish of the sea, and over the fowl of the air, and over every living thing that moveth upon the earth." The human race has a cooperative task. The social order prospers in proportion to our willingness and ability to work together toward a common goal.

The Dignity of Work

The dignity of work has lost much of its meaning in an industrial age where so many jobs are mechanical. It is difficult to see the image of God reflected in sitting and pushing a button all day. Perhaps it can only be recovered in the realization that the person is a part of a larger group who together are producing something worthwhile.

Labor and Management

Many of the tensions of society issue from the world of work when there is not the proper communication or appreciation between labor and management. Too often labor is thought of as an expendable force which makes the machinery of industry run. Laborers are not always treated as human beings worthy of consideration but as digits to be exploited in the interest of the company. Management, on the other hand, is often despised by labor as villians who sit on their summit, sopping up the gravy, enjoying an inordinate percentage of the profits for a minimum of effort.

There must be labor and management. They are both essential to the work force. But somehow they need to strive toward a better understanding and mutuality in their relationship. They need to learn to be "laborers together with God" as they fulfill their part in society's work ethic.

Strabo, the famous Greek geographer, wrote that the ancient Iberians were very brave warriors, but they often lost the battle because they never learned to hold their shields together in battle. They fought bravely, but every man was for himself. Their enemies defeated them because of superior teamwork. The human race thrives as we learn to hold our shields together to work in unison for the good of all.

Our Brother's Keeper

Cain's question, "Am I my brother's keeper?" brings to light another aspect of man's social nature. The lesson taught in the story of Cain and Abel is that we are responsible for each other as God's special creation. Complete individuality is a violation of God's creative intent. We cannot be responsible to God without being responsible for our fellow human beings. We are all kinsmen in the flesh and in the spirit. The mutual welfare of all is to be the concern of each.

God did not let the murder of Abel pass without accountability. He who knows the fall of the sparrow also knows the human hurts and abuses. He holds the human race responsible for the injustices, the inequities, and inhumanities. We are our brothers' keepers.

I once read an article in a Dallas, Texas, newspaper about a man who began shouting, "Nobody loves me!" and then walked into the middle of a busy intersection, lay down in the street, and awaited oncoming traffic. Presently he was struck by a station wagon whose driver did not see him. His death was ruled a suicide. An identification card showed his address as 2022 Lonesome Circle. There are many people who live on Lonesome Circle, feeling that nobody loves them. Perhaps the man's death was not so much suicide as homicide by a society that tends to forget it is responsible for its brother.

Individualized Concern

The trend today is toward social welfare agencies assuming this brotherly burden. We expect that the government or some community agency will meet the need. There simply aren't enough funds to stretch that far. Furthermore, assistance often becomes bogged down in the red tape of regulations. Nothing takes the place of a caring fellow human being who extends a loving hand to help. Jesus, in the parable of the good Samaritan, taught the importance of personal involvement in the plight of others. Institutional representatives passed by on the other side, but one compassionate individual stopped to render aid. John personalized this ministry of caring when he said, "But whoso hath this world's good, and seeth his brother have need, and shutteth up his bowels of compassion from him, how dwelleth the love of God in him?" (1 John 3:17). The selfish, disinterested person is denying the image of God in himself. The appropriate expression of divine compassion is suggested in the words of Mrs. Frank A. Breck: "Look all around you, find some one in need, Help somebody today!"

World Hunger

One of the most pathetic social situations in our world is the starving millions. Whether the hungry live in our community or half a world away, they are fellow beings who deserve our pity and our forthright action to put bread in their mouths. A study of the National

Academy of Science reports that 750 million people in the poorest nations live in extreme poverty with annual incomes of less than seventy-five dollars. It reports that at least 462 million people are actually starving. About 40 thousand human beings die each day after a painful period of starvation. About half of those are estimated to be children. This does not reflect well upon man's concern for his fellow-man. Created in the image of God presupposes that we cannot look upon our unfortunate brothers without seeking to relieve their needs. The divine image can be overshadowed, however, by strictly human lethargy and indifference. I read about a missionary who went to India and was so appalled at the misery all about, he could scarcely eat. After a time he found that he could step over the dead and dying on the sidewalk without paying much heed. He became so disturbed at his own insensitivity he prayed, "Lord, help me to care." This is an appropriate prayer for those who bear the divine imprint.

Racial Discrimination

Paul, in his speech to Council of the Areopagus, declared that God "hath made of one blood all nations of men for to dwell in all the face of the earth" (Acts 17:26). This was Paul's interpretation of the Genesis account as far as the races of men were concerned. Human beings are human beings whatever the color of the skin, the slant of the eye, or the other superficial differences. They are equal in dignity, for the image of God is equally distributed to all. This truth is violated when society is fragmented into groups which hold belittling or hostile attitudes toward each other. Racism is ugly because it denies the essential worth of every person before God.

Units in Society

There are legitimate and natural units in which people identify with other people. For its proper functioning, the human race falls into divisions that are conducive to human growth and usefulness.

The Family

The family is the first relationship according to the design of God. God did not simply create individuals but a family. He could just as well have made two men or two women, but, instead, He created them male and female. The basic unit of society, then, is the family. The first humans, according to the creation account, were made full-grown. Even so, they needed a relationship that was intimate and caring. Only then could their creative potential of personhood be fulfilled. The maleness and the femaleness could be expressed in a permanent union that had infinite possibilities, including the repro-duction of their own kind. Family provides the means of perpetuation of the race under the most desirable conditions. The lengthy span of childhood demands a stable situation where the child can be nour-ished, protected, and trained to face life on his or her own. Values and culture are transmitted in the family unit. I doubt that the human race could have survived, certainly not have prospered, without the family. The family is an external womb corresponding to the warmth and security of the prenatal womb of the mother.

Society, then, was not by chance or choice. God conceived of man living in association as the necessary condition of realizing all that the divine image implied.

The importance of the family to the well-being of society cannot be overemphasized. At a time when the divorce rate is almost equal to the marriage rate, there is reason to be alarmed. The validity of the traditional family is being challenged by those who minimize the need for marriage or, at least, think of it as a temporary expedient. Couples are playing family by living together in a union of convenience that has no lasting commitment. If the family is indeed the basic social unit, it would seem that the foundations of society are being shaken.

One of the greatest contributions that Christians can make to the welfare of mankind is to cherish the principles upon which God established the family, that of an enduring and endearing relationship through life. This is in keeping with the intent of God and the best interests of the human race. It is through a stable and happy family environment that the image of God in man can best be brought to its fullest flower.

The Clan

As the family of Adam increased, it began to diversify. The sons of Adam became the centers for additional groupings that were an extended expression of the family of man. Cain, for example, as a result of the strife with Abel, "went out from the presence of the Lord, and dwelt in the land of Nod, on the east of Eden" (Gen. 4:16). Jabal "was the father of such as dwell in tents, and of such as have cattle" (v.20). His brother Jubal "was the father of all such as handle the harp and organ" (v.21). Tubal-cain was "an instructor of every artificer in brass and iron" (v.22). Clans began to form of multiple family groups identified by kinship, locale, trade, and the like. Much later in Israel's history, this found expression in the tribal groupings. The twelve tribes of Israel formalized in the land of Egypt, perhaps in an effort not to lose their Hebrew identity in an alien country. These twelve tribes came together and cooperated in forming a nation once they arrived in the Promised Land.

When Christianity came along and tribal distinctions lost their meaning, the church itself provided a society in which the followers of Christ could find identity and relationship with their own kind. In this community of belief and worship, the Christian realizes the richest appropriation of his faith and fellowship with God. The person who seeks to live in spiritual isolation usually has a distorted image of God. We need our fellow Christians, both those who are now living and also those who preceded us, to properly grasp the divine revelation and to cultivate the image of God in ourselves. The foundation of the church by our Lord gives recognition to the social aspect of man's nature.

I once read an illustration about a pastor who was visiting a church member who seldom attended worship. The member suggested to the pastor that he could be just as good a Christian without going to church. They were seated in front of a fireplace. The pastor, in answer, took a poker and drew from the fire a single glowing ember. Presently the glow began to diminish. The pastor hoped the parishioner got the point. Something happens when people are in association. They mutually stimulate each other and share the fire of their spiritual reality.

One of the most chilling words in our vocabulary is the word *alone*. Even the most reclusive people ordinarily need a few friends. Ulysses S. Grant was a loner, according to a recent biographer, but seemed to "have been terrified by being alone."[2] Although he commanded thousands of men during the Civil War, he needed a handful of men around him to help him keep command of himself.

What the World Needs Now

As much as man needs human association, he has tendencies that often make relationships difficult. He has very strong selfish inclinations that create breaches between him and others. This is vividly illustrated in the Genesis story. Adam and Eve were moved by selfish considerations to disobey God. The beautiful intimacy they had enjoyed with the Creator was interrupted, and they were sent from His presence. Sin builds barriers between the individual and God so that this most essential social expression is forfeited.

In an act of selfishness and spite, Cain slew his brother Abel. In the aftermath, Cain left the family unit and went to dwell in lonely exile. When our relationship with God is not good, it is more difficult to establish enduring human associations. The most disruptive factors in society are selfishness and pride. More than anything else, these two things break up marriages and friendships. The conflicts in society have their roots in sinful human nature. The one hope of bringing these social disruptions under control is fellowship with God. Selfishness and pride are in direct contradiction to the image of God in man. Love is the primal attribute of deity and, thus, also the most appropriate expression of the divine likeness. In relationship with God, that love is cultivated and liberated to express itself in social contacts. The ugly aspects of human nature are subdued. The popular song of recent years was correct when it said, "What the world needs now is love, sweet love." As love flourishes, so do peaceful and happy human associations. Love is the only thing that can relieve the hostility that causes clans to line up against other clans and families to bring disintegration. Love fosters tolerance and acceptance of those who differ from us. Patience and kindness are social lubricants applied by love.

Jesus came emphasizing the importance of the dual affection. "Thou shalt love the Lord thy God. . . . and thy neighbour as thyself" (Matt. 22:37-39). In loving God, we are free to love one another and to live by the golden principle of social goodwill, "Therefore all things whatsoever ye would that men should do to you, do ye even so to them" (Matt. 7:12). Here lies the secret of social harmony.

Notes

1. Norman and Jeanne MacKenzie, *H. G. Wells* (New York: Simon Schuster, 1973), p. 413.

2. William S. McFreely, *Grant* (New York: W. W. Norton & Co., 1981), p. 87.

9
Created Free

Adam and Eve were created free. God placed them in a safe and sufficient environment where their needs were met. He placed only one prohibition upon them. They were not to eat of the tree of the knowledge of good and evil, which was in the midst of the garden. Why would God impose a solitary restriction upon those to whom He had given such liberty? Is it somewhat unfair on the part of the Creator to have made such a tree in the first place and to have subjected Adam and Eve to this sort of temptation?

The answer, I believe, is found in the consideration of the image of God in man. God is sovereign. He is absolutely free to act according to His will and purpose. If man partakes of the divine image, then he, too, must have some degree of sovereignty. He must be free to pick and choose in keeping with his own desires and designs. Unlike the beasts, he is not subject to the severe controls of instinct and a servant of his environment. He does have instincts, but God endowed him with a rational nature by which he evaluates his life circumstances. Man is able to exercise certain some control over his instincts and his environment.

Not a Robot

The human being, therefore, is a free moral agent. He does not enter the world completely programmed to behave by certain preordained patterns. Man has a capacity to act or not to act according to his own judgment or desire. In this sense, he is in the image of God and a true person. Personality involves the privilege and the ability to make choices. This freedom is not real unless there is an opportunity to

135

make wrong choices as well as good ones. Eden would have been a very glamorous prison if the first man and woman had been so protected that they could not exercise their personhood. God would have been manipulating them to the point that they had no true personhood. None of the attributes associated with the image of God would have been able to surface. Man would have existed in a bubble of innocence but never realized his humanity.

The Opportunity to Choose

The purpose of the tree of the knowledge of good and evil becomes clear as we interpret it from the viewpoint of man's freedom to choose. The divinely endowed capacity would have meant nothing and would have withered away without opportunity to express itself. God placed the tree in the midst of the garden to elicit from these first human representatives the exercise of their freedom of choice. Only in this way would their personhood blossom.

It seems a considerable risk upon the part of God that He should have allowed this decision. The stakes were very high because God said that they should not eat "lest you die." There was also the chance that they would abuse the freedom and make the wrong choices. There was no alternative if man were to be created in the image of God. Parents undergo something of this same peril in producing children. There is always the chance that they might bring into the world a defective child or one who would grow up to be a menace to society. Prospective parents also know that there is a possibility that their child might be healthy and mature into a responsible person. God created the human race with the same built-in gamble.

In the Image of God

Elton Trueblood has said that the image of God in man is in man's power of choice. As I have interpreted the image in terms of personhood, it seems that freedom is simply one magnificent aspect of the image. Man could not be like God in any way, however, if there were not the liberty of action. In this he partakes of the very essence of God. The ultimate expression of that freedom is the ability to deny or defy God. Man can say yes or no to God, the divine Creator and Lord of all the universe. Indeed, this is freedom in its most absolute form. Man in this respect is his own personal sovereign. He can do what he pleases whether it is in harmony with the divine will or serves his best interests.

Limitations to Freedom

To speak of limitations in respect to freedom may seem like a contradiction. However, we need to remember that God in His freedom imposed a limitation upon Himself in making man free. He gave the human beings a capacity to oppose Him, and God would respect that opposition. He, therefore, surrendered some of His sovereignty in making humans in His own image. God does not dictate how that freedom may be used. Even His grace may be resisted.

The expression of freedom is conditioned by many factors, including our personalities, likes and dislikes, heredity, education, and environments. Adam and Eve's desire was greatly influenced by their own appetites and by the enticements of the serpent. Freedom is not, therefore, exercised in a vacuum. Seldom is a person free to do exactly what he or she pleases at any given moment. We are even compromised by previous decisions.

The Christian, for example, has made a commitment to Christ that strongly influences his subsequent choices. He is free to do anything he wants with his life, but his encounter with Christ predisposes him to choose a life of decency and honor. This does not mean that freedom is not real but that the exercise of our choices is influenced by our total situation. Like the Heavenly Father, in our freedom we choose to impose limitations upon ourselves, for example, by the acceptance of Christ as our Savior. It is a kind of reverse action corresponding to God's restraint of sovereignty.

God Never Coerces Man

In recognition of the freedom in which He created man, God never imposes His will upon us. Even Jesus, praying in Gethsemane, seemed to have an alternative. The agony of that garden experience would not have been real unless Jesus were actually grappling with a decision. It was God's plan and will that Jesus should go to the cross, but Jesus had to go by His personal choice if He were truly to be our sin-bearer. When Jesus prayed, "Thy will be done," an angel from heaven appeared, strengthening Him. When we make the correct decisions, the Heavenly Father will encourage and assist us.

When I finished high school, I planned to attend a teachers' college on a scholarship I had received. I knew in my heart that God wanted me to preach, but thus far I was exercising my freedom to ignore the call. A youth revival led by a seminary student named John Newport came to our town just before school was to start. Through my association with those fine young people, I found the courage and inspiration to say yes to God. God will call but not coerce. He will touch your heart but not twist your arm. In that sense, we choose our own destiny.

Live with Consequences

We are free to choose our courses in life, but we are not free to choose the consequences. Adam and Eve had been warned of the danger in partaking of the forbidden fruit but listened to the arguments of the serpent and, supposing they could eat with impunity, disobeyed God. That was their privilege. God gave them the prerogative of making the choice. They did not, however, have any control over the evil consequences that resulted from the choice. They were thrust from the garden and from the presence of the God who had blessed them with His own image.

I went into a small place of business one day to visit with the owner. Immediately, he closed and locked the door. He was despondent and needed to talk. He told me that when he was a young man God had called him to preach. He had rejected the call. He said, "My business is failing; my home is breaking up; and I am so miserable, and I know why. Because I said no to God's call." I felt that his unhappiness would have been mine if I had not acceded to God's leadership in my life. He had the freedom to defy God but not the freedom to determine the aftermath.

Difficulty in Surrendering Sovereignty

Man is a sovereign person. He is the captain of his soul. No one, not even God, can make decisions for him unless he allows it. This can easily lead to an egotism in which pride becomes his master. "Ye shall be as gods," said the serpent. "Don't let anyone tell you what you can and can't do," the serpent was saying. "Be your own person." This is still a natural impulse that often leads the human race into terrible pitfalls. The greatest struggle with Christianity is that it requires a surrender of sovereignty. In submission to Christ, the person is forfeiting the right to run his own life. The believer freely chooses to follow God's will.

God would not be content with any other commitment than that which is given freely. Only in this way can there be face-to-face fellowship between two sovereign persons: God, who set limits some of His freedom when He made man free, and man, who surrenders some of his freedom when he accepts Christ as Savior.

Accepting Responsibility for Choices

A part of the maturing process is the acceptance of responsibility for our decisions. Adam and Eve tried to shift the guilt for a wrong decision to someone else. Adam blamed Eve, and Eve, in turn, accused the serpent. In fact, Adam even tried to implicate God, for he said, "The woman whom thou gavest to be with me, she gave me of the tree, and I did eat" (Gen. 3:12). In other words, it was God's fault in giving him the woman in the first place. Eve declared, "The serpent beguiled me, and I did eat" (v.13). Adam and Eve knew better than partake of the forbidden fruit. They just didn't do better, and they were defending their poor judgment. We often try to find convenient scapegoats for our errors of choice, but this does not negate personal responsibility.

Mark Twain wrote a book called *What Is Man?* He had a very dismal viewpoint of mankind. He declared that life has no dignity or meaning and each member of the human race is driven wholly by self-interest, the need to conform, the need, above all others, for peace of mind, for spiritual comfort. "Man's proudest possession, his mind, is a mere machine, an automatic machine," he declared.

Bernard DeVoto wrote in reply, "No one can read this wearisomely repeated argument without feeling the terrible force of an inner cry: Do not blame me, for it was not my fault."[1]

"Don't blame me," is an infantile echo from Eden which we are inclined to repeat. God won't allow us to lay the blame on anyone except ourselves for the unwise use of our freedom. It is only when we accept the personal responsibility for our choices that we make amends with God and mature into our full personhood.

Was the Image Lost When Man Fell?

This question has been wrestled with by Bible students through the ages. Some have felt that the image of God in man was forfeited when Adam and Eve disobeyed God and were expelled from Eden. They have thought this way because of a limited understanding of "image" and, also, because the New Testament seems to teach that in Christ the image is recovered. There are passages, however, that imply that mankind, generally, is in the image of God, both redeemed and un-redeemed. First Corinthians 11:7 says, "For a man indeed ought not to cover his head, forasmuch as he is the image and glory of God." Genesis 9:6, long after the fall, speaks of man in the image: "Whoso sheddeth man's blood, by man shall his blood be shed: for in the image of God made he man." In other words, manslaughter violates the dignity of man made in the image of God.

The image of God in man, as we have seen, refers to his personhood, which distinguishes the human being from the animal world. The image is an essential aspect of personhood. At the fall, man did not cease being man. He retains the attributes that we associate with human personality, such as self-awareness, God-awareness, individuality, rationality, and morality. He does not become a beast. He is still a human.

What Did Man Lose in the Fall?

For one thing, man lost innocence. This is symbolized in the shame Adam and Eve felt about their naked bodies. For the first time, human beings felt a sense of guilt and sought to hide from God. Their eyes were opened to the moral and spiritual implications of disobeying God. To obey God made them feel good; to disobey God made them feel awful. Sin became a painful reality in human life.

The second thing man lost was life. God said, "In the day that thou eatest thereof, thou shalt surely die" (Gen. 2:17). Obviously, Adam and Eve did not die physically at that moment of eating. The death they experienced must have had implications other than physical. The most noticeable aftermath was the loss of the intimate relationship with God. They were sent forth from the garden where they had enjoyed such beautiful fellowship with the Creator. Cherubim stood guard at the gate with flaming swords to keep Adam and Eve away from the tree of life. The tree of life, no doubt, suggests life at its best, life in happy relationship with deity, blessed of God forever. To lose that kind of fellowship with the Heavenly Father is the essence of spiritual death.

Paul in Romans 1:21 described the coarsening effects of sin in human life. "For although they knew God, they neither glorified him as God nor gave thanks to him, but their thinking became futile and their foolish hearts were darkened" (NIV). When human beings disavow God, they lose their spiritual orientation. The spiritual aspects of the divine image become blunted. If they persist in this sinful direction, they can scarcely tell the difference between light and darkness, good and evil, truth and falsehood.

I once wrote an evangelistic tract entitled *The Rapture of the Deep.* The expression comes from scuba diving in which a person with the aid of a breathing device can explore the underwater world. There is a danger, however, that one can go so deep that he is overcome by a kind of narcosis or euphoria. It is called "rapture of the deep." He may remove his mouthpiece under the illusion that he can swim about freely like a fish. He may become giddy to the point that he doesn't know whether he is going up or down and may descend to his death. I made the point that one can go so deep into sin that one loses all sense of moral responsibility. One can't tell the difference between right and wrong. Powers of spiritual perception are diminished to the dangerous degree that one may never be able to come back.

Will and Ariel Durant wrote *A Dual Autobiography.* This famous writing team explored together the realm of philosophy and history. Ariel confessed that, as she began to turn her investigation inward, she was dumbfounded at what she discovered. "My hands shake as I grope into the jungle of the past and find the sources of that troubled stream which is my life. There has been so much chaos in me; there have been so many absurdities and mistakes, so many unreconciled elements of good and evil."[2]

"So much chaos in me" expresses very well the tragic situation that evolves in human life when the person is away from God. There is confusion, distortion, ugliness, guilt, and hopelessness. Man is out of his element. He was made by God for God in God's image. Chaos becomes order only when people find their way through Christ back to the intimate fellowship with God in the garden.

Choosing to Choose

This freedom to choose can sometimes be fearsome and threatening. There are people who would prefer to exist in a decisionless world. A recently married man confessed to me that sometimes he wished he were back on his father's farm where each day his dad could tell him what to do. Some people retreat from the responsibility of making decisions by choosing to identify with some authoritarian government, society, or religion which asks only their conformity. This course fixes the individual in a state of perpetual immaturity. Full selfhood is never realized.

Parents should be careful to allow their children to develop in the area of choice making. If the child is to be a responsible adult, he must learn early in life to make good choices. A man was installing a television antenna on the roof of his house. He heard a fluttering noise in a tree nearby. A young bird was dangling upside down below the nest. Its leg was entangled in a piece of string that had been used to build the nest. The man eased along the roof until he could cut the string and put the bird back in the nest. Parents can innocently attach so many strings to their children that they can actually inhibit their personality development. Children need guidance but not smothering. The strings can be cut by encouraging them to accept the responsibility of making decisions. Only then can they become free men and women.

The Church Fostering Freedom

Joshua long ago set the stage for religious freedom when he said, "Choose you this day whom ye will serve; whether the gods which your fathers served that were on the other side of the flood, or the gods of the Amorites, in whose land ye dwell: but as for me and my house, we will serve the Lord" (Josh. 24:15). It is never recorded that Jesus compelled anyone to follow Him. He gave the invitation, but the choice was left to the individual. God in the flesh could hardly have done otherwise and have been true to His creative purpose, that of making man a free moral agent. Coercion in spiritual matters is inconsistent with the image of God in man. Each individual must have the privilege of deciding for himself the spiritual direction of his life.

Churches that practice a kind of proxy religious confession violate this creative principle. More in line with human freedom is the doctrine of the "priesthood of the believers." This simply means that no one can act for me in my relation to God. Each person has access to God and must make his own religious decisions. In the zeal to make converts, congregations are sometimes manipulated by skilled evangelists to make decisions that are not real. Such persons may then be subject to disillusionment in which they come to believe that Christianity is a farce. It is proper to create a climate for assent to the leadership of the Spirit and then to permit the worshiper to make a free choice.

The Basic Freedom

Freedom of choice in respect to religious expression is the basic freedom. Liberty in all other areas flows from this fount. It recognizes the dignity of human life and that man was meant to freely choose his own destiny. When human oppression arises, it attacks, first of all, the religious rights. Communism is a zealous opponent of Christianity because it knows that free men cannot be compressed into a complaint lump of humanity.

G. K. Chesterton once said, "There is no basis for democracy except in the dogma about the divine origin of man." America has become the home of the free largely because of Christian idealism. Roger Williams was dismayed when he left the Old World with its tyranny to find in the colonies a similar oppression in the name of Christianity. He had grasped the truth that God intended all men to have freedom of choice, and he founded Rhode Island Colony, where this principle could be officially practiced. This ideal of freedom implanted itself in colonial leaders and eventually became the prevailing spirit of America.

In 1940, when the Jefferson Memorial was being erected in Washington, D.C., an assistant to Harold Ickes, Secretary of the Interior, went to view the edifice. He returned to his office and expressed his disappointment to Mr. Ickes. He bemoaned the fact that a monument was being built to honor one of the greatest champions of liberty and one of the most versatile writers of his time, and yet there was not a single sentence of Jefferson's inscribed on his monument. Mr. Ickes charged the man to search the writings of Jefferson and discover some appropriate words of the statesman. He placed on Mr. Ickes' desk one day words of the patriot that expressed Jefferson's commitment to freedom, and today they are found on the monument: "I have sworn upon the altar of God, eternal hostility against every form of tyranny over the mind of man."

Arnold Toynbee once said, "I believe that man cannot live without freedom. His spiritual life is the sphere in which he needs freedom most of all. And religion may be the only field left for freedom of any kind in the world into which we are moving."

The Founding Fathers of America realized that religion was vital to the national welfare. In Washington's Farewell Address to Congress, he said, "Whatever may be conceded to the influence of refined education on minds of peculiar structure, reason and experience both forbid us to expect that national morality can prevail in exclusion of religious principle." John Adams wrote, "Without religion, the world would be something not fit to be mentioned in polite company . . . I mean hell." He also said, "Statesmen may speculate liberty, but it is religion or morality alone upon which freedom can securely stand. A patriot must be a religious man."

Separation of Church and State

As our nation began to take shape, the leaders began to realize that for real freedom to exist, there must be a separation of church and state. They never intended to disdain or exclude religion but to assure its free expression. Furthermore, they recognized that the state must be spared the religious entanglements which had existed in Europe. The churches have prospered in this atmosphere of freedom, and the nation has been blessed by their influence.

Constant vigilance is needed, however, lest this freedom be lost because of political maneuvering or pressures of self-interested church groups. Sometimes enormous campaigns are waged by religious bodies to bring to pass legislation in favor of their particular viewpoints. Politicians in the effort to gather votes may cater to these groups.

Charles Colson, who was once in President Nixon's inner circle, wrote an article in which he described how religious leaders were often invited to the White House, where they were buttered up and flattered in an effort to sway their thinking and elicit their support for the president and his party. Freedom can be forfeited almost unconsciously if we are not sensitive to the subtle tugs from those in power. We have seen such things as prayer in public schools and abortion become emotional issues raised in presidential elections. Whenever the conviction of a certain religious community becomes incorporated into law, the freedom of the whole is curtailed.

Personal Habits and Freedom

Freedom is sometimes lost not just on the national front, but through personal practices that tend to enslave. Some habits, if followed long enough, bind the person in a way of life that is self-destructive and prevent him from being the free person God intended. Alcohol, for example, is addictive and holds in bondage millions of people who began drinking of free choice but no longer have that choice. Other drugs have made virtual zombies out of people created in the image of God. They have lost their dignity as persons and the freedom to exercise good judgment.

Some people who partake of destructive drugs do so under the illusion that they have inherent rights to do as they please. Freedom does not mean indulgence. Man created in the image of God violates his freedom when he does anything that mars the divine image. True freedom follows a responsible course. When one's behavior pattern is contrary to human dignity and desecrates that which is holy, it tends to enslave and to limit the exercise of freedom. Among other things, the health of the body and mind is destroyed, thus imprisoning the person in pain and frailty. The inability to cope with these debilitating substances destroys not just health but self-esteem. Many can never feel the exhilaration of the free and independent person God made them to be. They are captives to their own worst selves. Like Adam and Eve, they are victims of their own poor choices.

Whittier once wrote a poem about Daniel Webster, who he felt had disgraced himself by supporting the fugitive slave law. One of the stanzas reads:

> All else is gone; from those great eyes
>   The soul has fled;
> When faith is lost, when honor dies
>   The man is dead!

When people lose their sense of honor and dignity, indeed, they are reduced to nothing. We were created free, and it is our duty to remain free in every arena of life, religious, political, and personal. Only in that way do we pay respect to the God who made us in His image.

A Liberating Faith

Christianity is a liberating faith. It sets people free from powerful forces that inhibit and restrain. Jesus said, "Ye shall know the truth, and the truth shall make you free" (John 8:32). Christ came to restore to mankind the freedom which God originally bestowed upon him. Adam and Eve forfeited their freedom when they submitted to the enticements of the serpent. They immediately entered into the bondage of fear, guilt, shame, and a whole host of forces that snap padlocks on the human personality. One of the principle things which has intimidated man is a dread of God.

Throughout the ages the human race has sought ways to break out of this box. People have felt the necessity of placating God. They have created religions, fashioned idols, multiplied rules and regulations, none of which were capable of granting freedom. They were simply forging more chains to burden them. Christ came to strike away these chains and to free us to enjoy our relation with God. The liberty He gave us was one in which the human race came to realize that God is love and, all along, wants the very best for us.

Paul once admonished the Galatians, "Stand fast therefore in the liberty wherewith Christ hatch made us free, and be not entangled again with the yoke of bondage" (Gal. 5:1). The Galatians were in danger of interpreting Christianity as a legal matter in which their salvation depended upon obedience to certain rules and rituals.

Christianity is love. Living in the aura of love, God's love for us in Christ and our love for Him, is an experience of true freedom. This is life as God meant it for the creature He made in His own image. Any other way of life leads to bondage.

Notes

1. Justin Kaplan, *Mr. Clemens and Mark Twain* (New York: Simon and Schuster, 1966), p. 340.

2. Will and Ariel Durant, *A Dual Autobiography* (New York: Simon and Schuster, 1977), p. 11.

10
Christ Renewing the Image

The image of God in man is really the subject matter of the entire Bible. In the early chapters of Genesis, we read of God creating man in His own image and likeness. In other words, God endowed humanity with traits and characteristics akin to His own person and nature. We have discussed those attributes that identify man as a very special creature. Though he shares some of the physical aspects of the animal world, he became a living soul. He is a person as God is a Person. Only a person could share the characteristics of the divine Person, and only a person can have a relationship with God. Thus, in the garden of Eden we see man in his idyllic state, perfectly innocent and walking and talking with God. All the God-given attributes are functioning in perfect order.

Man's Moral Failure

The tranquility of Eden was shattered, however, by the invasion of sin. Through the deceitful enticements of the serpent, Adam and Eve disobeyed God's specific instruction and ate fruit of the forbidden tree of the knowledge of good and evil.

The serpent had appealed to their latent pride. "Ye shall be as gods," he said, "knowing good and evil" (Gen. 3:5). Adam's and Eve's disobedience introduced them into a new moral realm. Previously, good and evil were purely academic, but now their minds and consciences came alive to moral implications of their disobedience. They were enveloped in a spiritual gloom that frightened and depressed them. They had thought that partaking of the fruit would launch them on a grand ego trip, but instead it dropped them into a pit of despair. Immediately they knew that they had done wrong. For the first time, guilt plagued their consciences. They hid from God. Paradise was lost. They were thrust from the garden to eke out their living by their own ingenuity.

They did not lose the image of God, but it was considerably defaced. They retained those qualities necessary for personhood but forfeited two of the most important aspects of the image. They lost their innocence. They became guilt-ridden sinners, living in conscious disobedience to God's will. Secondly, they lost their relationship with God. Driven from the garden where they had enjoyed such intimacy with the Creator, they were on their own in a sometimes harsh and cruel world. A spiritual isolation and loneliness beset them. From that time forward, the human race experienced a homesickness for Eden and for the Father. The garden was off bounds, and God was out of reach. No yearning has assailed mankind like that of recovering fellowship with God.

Pride had reared its ugly head and led to their moral failure. Malcolm Muggeridge has pointed out that pride separates man from God and induces man to believe that he is God. Muggeridge says that the two sicknesses that afflict the human race are egomania and eratomania. Egomania is a fascination with self. Man becomes the center of his own world. Erato-mania is a consuming concern for the sensual aspects of life. Man wants things that make him feel good and satisfy his appetites.

Each human being born into the world inherits this willfulness and this craving for sensual satisfactions. We bear the mark of Adam in this respect. We find it easier to be bad than good. We imitate this ancestral disobedience to God in our desire to satisfy our egos and our yearnings.

In that respect, we have all "sinned, and come short of the glory of God" (Rom. 3:23). The glory of God is the splendor of His own divine Person. When God created people in His own image, He shared with them something of His own radiance. Man in his innocence was like a mirror reflecting that glory. When Moses came down from the mountain where he had been with God, his face shone with such glory it became necessary to put a veil over his face before the Israelites could look upon him.

Sin has veiled the countenance and the life of mankind so that the glory does not shine through. The double tragedy of sin is the loss of innocence and the loss of fellowship with God. In guilt, man is condemned to face life and destiny without God.

Has God Abandoned Man?

Did God reject the human race as a total failure? The history of God's dealings with humanity as revealed in the Bible displays the continuing concern of God. The Heavenly Father desperately wants to spare man from the ravages of sin and to enter again into fellowship with him. He has not given up on the human race.

Someone has pointed out that in other religions we have man's quest for God, but in the Bible we read about God's quest for man. Jesus defined His own ministry as that of seeking. "For the Son of man is come to seek and to save that which was lost" (Luke 19:10). Thus, He showed the truth of God's earnest effort to restore relationship. The parable of the prodigal son illustrates the eagerness with which God awaits man's homecoming.

Ed Sullivan, a famous television personality years ago, was a modern prodigal. He told of running away from home as a teenager. He almost starved to death in the city before notifying his brother of his whereabouts. His brother persuaded him to come home. As Sullivan approached home, he was intensely afraid of the reception he would receive from his father. Instead of rejection, it was the first time he ever saw his father cry. The Bible portrays God as tearfully doing all that He can to draw mankind back to Himself.

There is joy in heaven when a sinner repents. The reluctance for the sinner's return is on man's part, not God's. God reaches out in love to reclaim the only creature He made in His own image.

The Futility of Human Efforts

Through the ages, sinful mankind has been making pathetic efforts to undo the tragedy of Eden. People sense very keenly the alienation from God. Guilt drives them to desperate measures to restore harmony with God. In the Old Testament days, the Hebrews diligently performed their sacrifices and multiplied their laws. Religion was gradually reduced to a calculated formula of pious acts and careful observations of regulations. Jesus pronounced His verdict upon the efficacy of these rituals when He said, "Except your righteousness shall exceed the righteousness of the scribes and Pharisees, ye shall in no case enter into the kingdom of heaven" (Matt. 5:20).

To this very day, the idea still prevails that somehow people can remedy their spiritual predicament by their own efforts. Martin Luther long ago discovered the futility of seeking salvation by his own religious endeavors. He once wrote that he was a good monk and kept the rules of his order so strictly, "that I may say that if ever a monk got to heaven by his monkery, it was I." John Wesley came to America as a missionary to the Indians but came to realize that he could not fill the void in his own soul by doing good works. He cried, "I came to save the Indians, but, oh, who will save me?" Later at Aldersgate, his heart was strangely warmed by the truth that the "just shall live by faith."

At a country church where I was once pastor, the Sunday School superintendent came forward at a revival service to make a profession of faith in Christ. I was utterly amazed because I had assumed, in view of his service, that he was a Christian. Many are existing under the delusion that their spiritual needs are met by living a reasonably good life, belonging to a church, or worshiping with some regularity. By these acts they think they have removed the blight of Eden. The idea of self-salvation is probably the greatest heresy in Christendom. Most people who are not trusting Christ for salvation are counting on themselves. As Paul said, salvation is "not by works of righteousness which we have done" (Titus 3:5).

How is innocence to be restored once it is lost? Innocence is a state of absolute sinlessness. We cannot live one day without sin, let alone go back and undo all the sins of our past. A few years ago, a confused person greatly damaged the *Pieta,* a sculpture created by Michelangelo, displayed in Saint Peter's in Rome. Skilled artisans did their best to restore the work of art to its original state. The casual observer can hardly tell that damage has been done, but never can the *Pieta* be what it once was. Man has no skill to repair his life to the point of his original innocence. He can become better, but not perfect. He, therefore, remains a sinner.

Fellowship with God was lost when Adam and Eve sinned. A holy God and sinful man cannot exist together in a companionable relationship. The expulsion from Eden vividly illustrates this spiritual truth. The judgment of God upon sin is that of separation, immediate and eternal. Like Adam and Eve, every sinner is alienated from God by sin. The only way that fellowship can be renewed is by the removal of sin. Mankind is caught on a spiritual dead-end street. Because we are sinners, we cannot enter into desirable relationships with God, and we don't have the capacity to remove our sin. Are we, therefore, hopeless?

God Has a Plan

Before God created man, He certainly knew that this godlike creature would become a moral failure. Therefore, God already had a plan to reclaim humanity. Paul talked about this in Ephesians 1:4-5. "According as he hath chosen us in him, before the foundation of the world, that we should be holy and without blame before him in love: Having predestinated us unto the adoption of children by Jesus Christ to himself, according to the good pleasure of his will." God not only foresaw the fall but, also, had in His blueprints a plan for the reclamation of the human race. It was conceived in the love of God and carried out through Jesus Christ.

When the automobile manufacturers design a new automobile, they are aware that the car will sooner or later need repair. They provide for that by manufacturing and supplying dealers and mechanics with spare parts so the car can be fixed. In somewhat the same way, the Author of our being conceived a plan to renew mankind before He created us and put that plan into action at the very outset of human life.

In Genesis 3:15, we have an intimation of this great truth. God pronounced a curse upon the serpent for having been the instrument for leading Adam and Eve astray. Then the Lord said, "I will put enmity between thee and the woman, and between thy seed and her seed; it shall bruise thy head, and thou shalt bruise his heel." Theologians sometimes speak of Genesis 3:15 as the gospel in its first elementary expression. The idea in the verse is that of continual conflict between good and evil. But the descendants of Eve will render a vital blow to evil in the crushing of the serpent's head. Many interpreters feel that this prophecy anticipates the coming of Jesus, who would bring the battle with evil to a mighty climax on the cross. In His death, the victory over evil would be won, making possible the restoration of man's fellowship with God. At least we find in this verse the intimation of God's plan which was gradually revealed in time and history with the ultimate fulfillment in the life and ministry of Christ.

As far as the Bible is concerned, this is God's only plan. He has not provided alternate ways of salvation. A common error is the assumption that, if a person is earnest in his religious practice, the pathway he takes is not important. Peter made it plain that God has provided one Savior who alone can minister to our spiritual plight: "For there is none other name under heaven given among men, whereby we must be saved" (Acts 4:12).

Jesus Christ, God in the Flesh

When Jesus Christ was born at Bethlehem, the preliminaries were over. At last, God was putting into action the plan He had conceived before the world was made. The curtain was drawn on the final act of the drama of redemption. Because the human race was totally impotent when it came to renewing themselves, God in His power and grace set in motion events that would make possible the restoration of man to Eden's flawlessness and the intimacy of Eden's fellowship with the Creator.

The Bible reveals that Jesus Christ was God incarnate, that is, Jesus was God in human flesh. "And the Word was made flesh, and dwelt among us (and we beheld his glory, the glory as of the only begotten of the Father,) full of grace and truth" (John 1:14). Paul beautifully sets forth this truth in Philippians 2:6-8:

> Who, being in very nature God,
> did not consider equality with

> God something to be grasped,
> but made himself nothing,
>> taking the very nature of a servant,
>> being made in human likeness.
> And being found in appearance as a man,
>> he humbled himself
>> and became obedient to death—
>>> even death on a cross! (NIV).

In Christ, God Himself walked on the stage of human history. This identity of Jesus with God was the real basis of His conflict with the Jewish leadership. It also became the crux of the dispute between the gospel defenders and the gospel detractors in the early Christian centuries. Jesus maintained in His own teaching that He was truly God. "I and my Father are one" (John 10:30). To Philip, Jesus explained, "He that hath seen me hath seen the Father" (John 14:9).

The apostle Paul wrote Colossians, in part, to assure the Christians of Christ's deity because they were harassed by false teachers who denied this tenet. He described Jesus as the divine Savior,

> who is the image of the invisible God, the firstborn of every creature: For by him were all things created, that are in heaven, and that are in earth, visible and invisible, whether they be thrones or dominions, or principalities or powers: all things were created by him, and for him. And he is before all things and by him all things consist (Col. 1:15-16).

There is no doubt that Paul believed Jesus to be God in person.

John in his letters demanded this same conviction on the part of those who were truly Christian. "And we know that the Son of God is come, and hath given us an understanding, that we may know him that is true, and we are in him that is true, even in his Son Jesus Christ. This is the true God, and eternal life" (1 John 5:20).

A battle raged in the early Christian centuries over the manner in which Jesus was related to God. Some theologians said that Jesus was like God but not really God. Others maintained that Jesus was the same as God. He was of like substance with God. This issue was settled for most Christians at the Council of Nicea in AD 325. Jesus Christ was declared to be of "one essence" with the Father.

This conviction about Christ as the Son of God who came into the world to live among us as a human being was formally expressed in the Apostles' Creed. Although not written by the apostles, it has been recited from ancient times in some church communions as a capsuled confession of basic Christian faith. At the outset it reads, "I believe in God the Father Almighty, and in Jesus Christ his only begotten Son, our Lord, who was born of the Holy Ghost, and the Virgin Mary."

Jesus Christ, the Ideal Man

In the beginning, God created man in His own image and likeness. In other words, He bestowed upon humanity His own personhood. This unique quality of life in man made possible the incarnation, the assuming of human form by Jesus Christ. Because Jesus Christ is a person, He could only be revealed in personhood. Inasmuch as He was both God and man, He could reflect in His humanity the nature of God.

Time after time the New Testament speaks of Jesus as the image of God. Paul said, "Christ, who is the image of God" (2 Cor. 4:4). We have already seen that in Colossians 1:15 Paul described Jesus as being the "image of the invisible God." The author of Hebrews left no doubt as to the identity between the Son and the Father, "who being the brightness of his glory, and the express image of his person" (Heb. 1:3).

The word "image" (*eikōn*) as used in the New Testament concerning Jesus does not mean a resemblance. Jesus was not a mirror reflection of God. He was God. There was a perfect correspondence between the Son and the Father. So what we see of God in Jesus Christ is not a suggestion of what God is like. Jesus Christ was God in action. "He that hath seen me hath seen the Father" (John 14:9). Jesus Christ, therefore, fulfilled to a complete degree that image of God in man.

In Jesus, the image of God in human life is realized in its idealized form. This was possible in Christ as never in other humans because Christ is also God. In Christ was revealed flawless character, unbounded love, and faultless faith—all unattainable by sinful man.

Christ was the paragon of virtue, the unblemished example of human perfection. He is our ideal, never to be completely realized, but always to be diligently emulated.

Paul said, "For God, who commanded the light to shine out of darkness, hath shined in our hearts, to give the light of the knowledge of the glory of God in the face of Jesus Christ" (2 Cor. 4:6). He furthermore declared, "For in him dwelleth all the fulness of the Godhead bodily" (Col. 2:9). Man saw in Jesus Christ that glory from which he had fallen.

The Spiritual Goal of Man

We see in Jesus Christ the kind of person God wants us to be. He is the ideal and the goal of human destiny. The glory of Christ's person convicts us of the shabbiness of our own lives and also calls us to strive toward His perfection. God's intent from the beginning was that people should be like Jesus. Paul spoke of God's original plan in Romans 8:29, "For whom he did foreknow, he also did predestinate to be conformed to the image of his Son." Paul expressed his own commitment to this goal when he said, "For to me to live is Christ" (Phil. 1:21). Paul's spiritual efforts were in the direction of identifying with Christ so completely that it would be as though Christ were living through him.

One of the most widely distributed books of the twentieth century is Charles Sheldon's work *In His Steps.* The book encourages the Christian to be as Christlike as possible in daily life. We suffer severe limitations because we are not Christ, nor are we divine. Nevertheless, in our own bumbling way, we can all become more and more like Jesus if we really concentrate upon it and seek the help of the Holy Spirit. It is His task to re-create in us the likeness of Christ.

In becoming more like Jesus, we recover the image of God that has been obscured by our sin and rebellion. In the church of Saint Sophia in Istanbul, the ancient mosaics are being revealed. When the church fell into the hands of the Moslems, they plastered over the beautiful mosaics of Christ and other religious figures. In recent years, the plaster is being removed so that, once again, the beautiful works of Christian art are being viewed. In a similar way, the image of God comes to light as we get rid of the layers of evil and walk more and more in the steps of Jesus. We can accomplish this recovery only to a limited degree by our own efforts. Christ is not only the ideal but also has sent His Holy Spirit as the master craftsman who peels away the sin and repairs the damage to the image which sin has wrought.

Christ Paying Eden's Curse

In the garden of Eden, God pronounced a dreadful penalty upon sin. "In the day that thou eatest thereof thou shalt surely die" (Gen. 2:17). Disobedience to the express command of God brought spiritual tragedy upon humanity. The human race has continued to suffer the dreadful consequences of sin. The New Testament confirms the judgment for sin, "The wages of sin is death" (Rom. 6:23). A just God must judge sin and exact a penalty. God would not be God if He let people sin and get by with it. Death is an inevitable aftermath of sin. Recovery from sin's tragedy, therefore, involves the payment of sin's penalty.

On God's drawing board was a plan whereby the penalty could be assumed by another. That other one had to be a person who would willfully accept the responsibility and a person whose own life and character were morally spotless. Since no human being was equipped to fulfill that role, God took the problem on His own shoulders. He invaded the human domain through Jesus Christ. Jesus, because He was fully man, could face the temptations and trials of human beings and, because He was also God, could live the flawless life necessary for a redeemer. If Jesus had committed one sin, He would have been disqualified from dying for us. He would have had to suffer for His own sin.

But one day on Calvary, Jesus submitted voluntarily to suffer the indignities of a criminal's death that the penalty imposed at Eden might be satisfied in behalf of all humanity. The justice of God was vindicated in the death of Jesus. An answer had been found to remove Eden's curse. John 3:16 sums up the gracious act of God in our behalf. "For God so loved the world, that he gave his only begotten Son, that whosoever believeth in him should not perish, but have everlasting life." Or, as Paul said, "God made him who had no sin to be sin for us, so that in him we might become the righteousness of God" (2 Cor. 5:21, NIV).

The Recovery of the Image

The road to recovery was blazed by Christ when He died for us on the cross. We step on that road when we commit ourselves to the living Christ in an experience of repentance and faith. The death penalty is removed from each individual who deposits his trust in Christ as his Savior.

Paul put it like this, "There is therefore now no condemnation to them which are in Christ Jesus, who walk not after the flesh, but after the Spirit" (Rom. 8:1). He continued to say that Christ has made us free from the law of sin and death. Our sentence has been nullified because someone paid the penalty in His own blood. We are on the way back to the garden when we are born again by God's grace and power.

Becoming a Christian is not just being rescued from the death penalty. It is, also, a life-changing, dynamic experience. Paul had this in mind in the words, "Therefore if any man be in Christ, he is a new creature: old things are passed away; behold, all things are become new" (2 Cor. 5:17).

Long ago God brought forth a new creature He called man. He endowed him with a personhood similar to His own Personhood. Man was created in the image of God. Very quickly this new, unique creature lost his spiritual dignity and identity by rebelling against God. The image of God was marred and scarred. Every generation of man has sinned Eden's sin and ill reflected the divine image.

It takes a new creative act of God to restore the image. Through a spiritual birth, the likeness of God is renewed. Once again the glory of the Heavenly Father begins to shine through, as the ugliness of sin is removed. Joy Davidman, wife of C. S. Lewis, in speaking of her conversion, said that once she began her relation with Jesus Christ, she had a "sunny quality" about her personality. The Christian emerges from the darkness into light and begins to take on the characteristics of God seen in Jesus Christ.

Back to Paradise

Christ ministers in the Christian life in two very strategic areas so that man is ushered back into paradise. As we have observed, when man sinned against God, he lost his innocence before God and his fellowship with God. The unforgiven sinner cannot have an intimate relationship with God. As suggested by the experience of Adam and Eve, sin separates a person from God. Before that desired fellowship can be attained, the individual's sin must be blotted out.

Innocence is not recovered through Jesus Christ, for man is still a sinner. Innocence implies never having violated a moral command. Once innocence is lost, it is gone forever. That which Christ bestows is righteousness. He does so in response to our faith. Righteousness means that persons are made right with God. Their sins have been forgiven. They have new characters and new status before God. Because Christ assumed our guilt upon the cross, God receives us as though we were completely without sin. We become God's spiritual children and reflect this kinship through holy aspirations, lovingkindness, and moral integrity of our lives.

Access to God

One of the beautiful biblical words which applies to our new circumstance as Christian is "access." Paul characterized this new relationship with God in Romans 5:1-2: "Therefore being justified by faith, we have peace with God through the Lord Jesus Christ: By whom also we have access by faith into this grace wherein we stand, and rejoice in hope of the glory of God." Only the high priest had access to the holy of holies in the Temple. In remote times, the mercy seat resided in the holy of holies. The presence of God was experienced there in an unusual way. When Christ was crucified, the veil of the holy of holies was rent from top to bottom, symbolizing that in His death, all have direct access to God's presence and mercy through Christ.

Cherubim stood at the gate of Eden with flaming swords, allowing no access to its sanctuary. In a symbolic sense, when Christ becomes our Savior, the cherubim lower their swords, and the Christian gains entrance to the garden. The sin that separated him from God has been forgiven, for he is a new creature in Christ with the privilege of immediate fellowship with the Heavenly Father. That which was lost in Eden has been recovered.

A New Moral Power

The Love of Christ

The Christian has been declared righteous before God, and his calling is to live righteously. Two things give him a new moral power to reflect his divine origin in his daily life.

First of all, there is the love of Christ. Paul said, "The love of Christ constraineth us" (2 Cor. 5:14). There is a tremendous moral influence in our love of Christ and in the recognition of His love for us. Love is the greatest disciplinary force man knows. Elsa Maxwell once asked the Duchess of Windsor why she devoted so much time to her appearance. She replied that her husband gave up everything for her, including his throne. "If, when I enter a room, my husband can feel proud of me," she said, "that's my chief responsibility." Jesus Christ gave up everything, His celestial throne, His very life, for us. Surely our chief response to this love is to make Him proud of us.

The Presence of the Holy Spirit

The other new source of moral power is the presence of the Holy Spirit. The Holy Spirit helps the Christian stay oriented to Christian ideals. Paul contrasted two goals in life as the "things of the flesh" and the "things of the Spirit" (Rom. 8:5). The first way is the life centered in the material and sensual aspects, a way of life that ignores the image of God in man. The second way is that which sets one's affections on things above. It magnifies the spiritual aspects of life which is consistent with man's spiritual nature and his new life in Christ. The Holy Spirit leads us along the higher way.

The Holy Spirit's task is to bring the attributes of Jesus to full fruition in the Christian life. Paul identified these magnificent traits which were most completely revealed in the life and character of Jesus. He referred to them as the "fruit of the Spirit," in other words, the qualities of life the Spirit is seeking to produce in the Christian. "The fruit of the Spirit is love, joy, peace, longsuffering, gentleness, goodness, faith, Meekness, temperance" (Gal. 5:22-23). These are the characteristics of mature Christians. By cooperating with the Spirit, or as Paul said, "walking in the Spirit," we grow up in Christlikeness. "But we all, with open face beholding as in a glass the glory of the Lord, are changed into the same image from glory to glory, even as by the Spirit of the Lord" (2 Cor. 3:18).

Attaining Full Personhood

Newborn Christians have the potential of becoming more and more like Christ. This should be their goal and aspiration. Paul encouraged the Ephesian Christians to have this as their principle object. "Till we all come in the unity of the faith, and of the knowledge of the Son of God, unto a perfect man, unto the measure of the stature of the fulness of Christ: That we henceforth be no more children, . . . But . . . may grow up into him in all things" (Eph. 4:13-15).

As Christians developing in Christlikeness, we realize more and more what God designed us to be when He created persons in His own image. We are attaining full personhood. Since Christ is the full image of God, as we reflect Christlike characteristics, we are also revealing the image of God in us. We are fulfilling the divine intent in our creation.

Future Glory

No matter how earnest our efforts, we shall always fall short of Christlikeness. After all, He was God in flesh, and we are people in the flesh. Jesus was correct when He said, "The spirit indeed is willing, but the flesh is weak" (Matt. 26:41). Someone else has put it like this: "Heaven calls but earth clings." Our capacity for reflecting the divine image has definite human limitations. Paul felt the frustration but kept on striving to realize the ideal of living the perfectly Christlike life. But he had the impetus and inspiration of knowing that one day the goal would be attained in a fashion not then possible. John spoke of the sons of God and their future glory: "Beloved, now we are the sons of God, and it doth not yet appear what we shall be: but we know that, when he shall appear, we shall be like him, for we shall see him as he is" (1 John 3:2).

When Jesus Christ returns, Christians will experience a glorious transformation in which the image of God in man will reach its highest fulfillment. This will not exclude the body in its attainment. Remember that man in the complete sense is body and spirit, not simply a spirit inhabiting a body. Jesus Christ died upon the cross to redeem the entire person, body and soul. At death the spirit leaves the body, but not forever. The physical body returns to the elements from which God created it. But the full story is not told.

The Resurrection of the Body

When the Lord returns, the body will be reclaimed. The resurrection pertains to the bodily aspect of human life. Paul sought to allay the fears of the Thessalonian Christians about the welfare of those who had already died when Jesus returns. Christians who have died will return with Jesus, sharing His triumph.

Living Christians will have no priority over those who have died. Paul explained, "The dead in Christ shall rise first" (1 Thess. 4:16). Since the "dead in Christ" are accompanying Christ, Paul could not have meant that they shall be raised. He had reference to their bodies which perished. They will be brought forth from death, and there will be a reunion of body and spirit. The living will be caught up together with them to meet the Lord in the air. Presumably, the bodies of both the dead and the living undergo a significant transformation. (See 1 Thess. 4:13-18.)

In the fifteenth chapter of 1 Corinthians, Paul explained further what he meant by the resurrection. The body that is raised is not the same physical body that perished. "It is sown a natural body; it is raised a spiritual body" (v. 44). "The dead shall be raised incorruptible" (v. 52), that is, the resurrection body will not be subject to decay and the frailties of mortality. It will be a body suited for eternity. At this point, he said, "Death is swallowed up in victory." (v. 54) The human body will die. Death came in the aftermath of sin. However, in Jesus Christ, all the ravages of death are removed. The entire person, body and spirit, is preserved for eternity.

Immortality and Eternal Life

Man is a mortal creature by nature. Immortality belongs to God alone. He is the only Person in whom there is inherent life without any beginning or end. Every other creature, including man, must experience physical death. This is a part of the curse of God upon man for sin. Sin and death are defined as the two great enemies of mankind. Through Jesus Christ, man, the mortal creature, escapes the penalty of death. "Whosoever believeth on him . . . should have everlasting life" (John 3:16). Jesus, before raising Lazarus from the dead, pronounced to Martha the Christian's emancipation from death's tyranny. "I am the resurrection, and the life: he that believeth in me, though he were dead, yet shall he live: And whosoever liveth and believeth in me shall never die. Believest thou this?" (John 11:25-26).

In Christ's resurrection, all that man had in potential at Creation is fulfilled. All the godlike qualities emerge in complete form, including eternal life. The damage and tragedy of man's disobedience in Eden is completely remedied. Paradise is more than fully regained. In Revelation 22, John portrayed the destiny of God's people as a new Eden. He triumphantly announced, "And there shall be no more curse" (v. 3). The tree of life to which Adam and Eve lost access is available on both sides of the river. There is a universal invitation to every person excluded by sin from the blessings of God to come into the garden. "Come. . . . whosoever will, let him take the water of life freely" (v. 17).

But notice that the sovereignty of man in respect to his own personal will is not violated. "Whosoever will" recognizes that man, like God, has freedom of choice. No verse in the Bible, perhaps, so illuminates the dignity of man made in the image of God. He is free, but he is also responsible. He is not God, but a creature whom God designed for fellowship with Himself. He is a person as God is a Person, and God meant him to be a friend forever.

Who Am I?

We began this study by asking, What is man? It is appropriate to conclude with a more personal query, Who am I? A concerted effort is underway today to demonstrate that man is just a beast among beasts, an animal among animals, simply a more sophisticated representative of the animal kingdom. It has become a form of enlightenment to accept man's descent from the lower orders of animal existence. The understanding of the human being is enhanced, they say, by a penetrating study of primates who share a common ancestry with man. In the search for humanity's past, scientists are scratching around in the geological debris of remote ages. With delight, they expose a physical remnant of some prehistoric creature and announce that a human ancestor has been discovered. Man will never find himself or learn who he is in the boneyards of antiquity. For man is more than a physical phenomenon who appeared on earth at some undetermined time in the far distant past.

Who am I? The very fact I would ask that question reveals that I have characteristics beyond that of any non-human creature on earth. What other animal sits and puzzles over its identity? I am a unique and singular existence. I have abilities and traits not found in any consequence in other forms of life. Can it be that I simply evolved from some simple organism, molded only by nature's hands into an intelligent, sensitive, reflective human being? If so, why would nature concentrate such formative powers upon me alone?

When I sit on the beach and glory in the sunset, I am the only creature on earth who does so. When I bow my head in church to pray, no other animal joins me. When I sit at my typewriter to compose a letter or write a sermon or outline a book, I do so in solitary splendor.

There is something about me so special that I seem to have come from another world, produced by powers that particularized upon me. As I search for who I am, I find no answer so satisfactory as that which the Bible communicates. Somehow God implanted in the awareness of some ancient seer the truth unfolded in Genesis 1:27: "So God created man in his own image, in the image of God created he him; male and female created he them."

Something within me says amen to the words, "And the Lord God formed man of the dust of the ground, and breathed into his nostrils the breath of life; and man became a living soul" (Gen. 2:7).

At last I have found myself and understand myself. I don't have to gaze in bewilderment at fossilized remnants in a museum and wonder where I came from. God made me and made me very special. I am like other animals but more like God. I have possibilities that no other creature possesses. They are made for earth and time; I am made for heaven and eternity. They are made to serve man. I am made to serve God. They are creatures of instinct. I am a person who can walk and talk with my Maker.

I want to lift my face heavenward and praise God with the psalmist for the exalted state of the human race. What is man? "Thou hast made him a little lower than the angels, and hast crowned him with glory and honor. O Lord, our Lord, how excellent is thy name in all the earth!" (Ps. 8:5,9).

Scripture Index

167